# TAC: IN THE 1980s

Adrian Symonds

# Acknowledgements

I would like to thank Sally Tunnicliffe for her assistance. Special thanks go to my wife, Louise, and son, Charlie.

This book is dedicated to the men and women who served in Tactical Air Command.

First published 2021

Amberley Publishing
The Hill, Stroud
Gloucestershire, GL5 4EP

www.amberley-books.com



ISBN 978 1 4456 9858 8 (print)
ISBN 978 1 4456 9859 5 (ebook)



British Library Cataloguing in Publication Data.
A catalogue record for this book is available from the British Library.

Typesetting by SJmagic DESIGN SERVICES, India.
Printed in the UK.

# Contents

# The history and role of TAC

Tactical Air Command (TAC), headquartered at Langley Air Force Base (AFB), Virginia, was a major command (MAJCOM) of the United States Air Force (USAF) based almost entirely in the contiguous United States. Established on 21 March 1946 as a component of the Army Air Forces, it predated the USAF (established 18 September 1947) by eighteen months.

TAC was administratively organised into several Numbered Air Forces, controlling two for most of its history. By 1958 TAC had settled upon Ninth and Twelfth Air Forces (9th AF/12th AF), which were geographically focussed, respectively controlling units in the eastern and western halves of the contiguous United States. As well as 'combat-coded' units, TAC was responsible for conversion training of pilots and crews for aircraft types in the TAC inventory, therefore controlling several Replacement Training Units (RTUs) for this purpose.

Most TAC flying units were not intended to fight from their home bases in wartime. TAC's primary role was to hold a fleet of tactical combat aircraft that could rapidly deploy overseas, reporting to theatre commands rather than TAC HQ. Furthermore, Air National Guard (ANG) and Air Force Reserve (AFRES) tactical flying units were 'gained' by TAC if federalised/mobilised. TAC could then reallocate those units to relevant theatres as required. TAC's 9th/12th AF units routinely undertook worldwide deployments exercising their wartime role. During the 1980s the primary focus for wartime (and peacetime training) TAC aircraft deployments was to Europe, reinforcing United States Air Forces Europe (USAFE). Far East Asia (previously the primary focus during the Vietnam War period) remained an important deployment destination, reinforcing Pacific Air Forces (PACAF). The Middle East also became an increasingly important planning focus.

Due to Vietnam War budgetary pressures the F-4D equipped 49th Tactical Fighter Wing (TFW) was reassigned from USAFE to TAC in 1968. The wing was designated as 'dual-based', ready to immediately return to Germany in an emergency. This was regularly practiced under 'Crested Cap' exercises. After the 49th TFW took on the air superiority role with the F-15 in 1977, the F-4E equipped 4th TFW took over the 'Crested Cap' commitments. Further wings undertook the month-long 'Crested Caps' to West Germany from 1982. Other combat-coded TAC (and ANG/AFRES) units practiced their wartime USAFE reinforcement role, periodically making two-week 'Coronet' deployments to Europe, part of 'Checkered Flag' (a wider programme of practice deployments worldwide). While a number of reconnaissance units participated in 'Coronets', there were also 'Salty Bee' deployments to Europe exclusively for reconnaissance units.

Between 1955 and 1973 Nineteenth Air Force was assigned to TAC. This was task (rather than geographically) focussed. Unique in not having any units routinely assigned, it acted as the HQ for the Composite Air Strike Force (CASF). It was intended to rapidly deploy with assets transferred from 9th/12th AF to areas of the globe threatened by Communist aggression where US forces did not already have a footprint, such as Latin America or the Middle East. Tightening defence budgets as the Vietnam War wound down resulted in 19th AF inactivating in 1973, returning TAC to overseeing two Numbered Air Forces.

The 1979 Soviet invasion of Afghanistan highlighted the need to be able to deploy forces to the Middle East to counter any further Soviet moves in the region. The Rapid Deployment Joint Task Force (RDJTF) was activated on 1 March 1980 at MacDill AFB, Florida. Originally envisioned in the 1970s with a role of deploying a mobile task force of US Army, US Navy (USN), US Marine Corps (USMC) and USAF elements globally, the Soviet intervention in Afghanistan resulted in RDJTF having a focus on the Middle East and primarily the Persian Gulf region. RDJTF had no forces of its own; a number of US-based units from the four armed forces were earmarked for reassignment to its control as required. On 1 January 1983 United States Central Command (CENTCOM) activated, replacing RDJTF. Many of the TAC units earmarked for RDJTF/CENTCOM practiced deploying to the Middle East during the Bright Star exercises in Egypt. These were a consequence of the Camp David Accords and the first, 'Bright Star '81', took place from October to December 1980 (fiscal year 1981). Initially annual, they were subsequently held every other year.

TAC's 1980s backbone types: an A-10A leads an F-4E, an F-15A and an F-16A Block 10. All were from the 57th FWW at Nellis AFB. (National Archives and Records Administration)

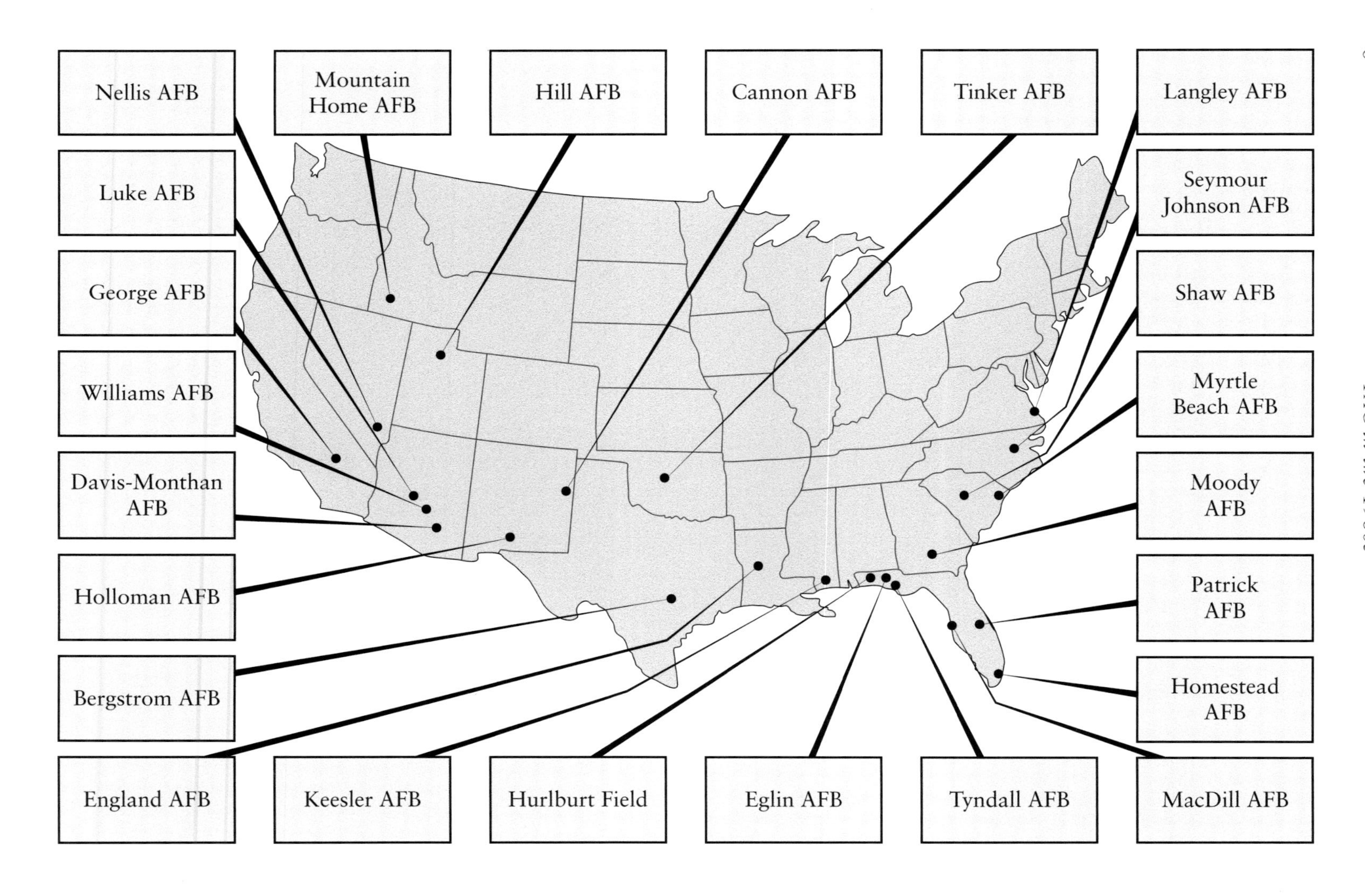
Nellis AFB
Mountain Home AFB
Hill AFB
Cannon AFB
Tinker AFB
Langley AFB
Luke AFB
Seymour Johnson AFB
George AFB
Shaw AFB
Williams AFB
Myrtle Beach AFB
Davis-Monthan AFB
Moody AFB
Holloman AFB
Patrick AFB
Bergstrom AFB
Homestead AFB
England AFB
Keesler AFB
Hurlburt Field
Eglin AFB
Tyndall AFB
MacDill AFB

Aerospace Defense Command (ADC), another USAF MAJCOM, had been responsible for providing strategic air defence forces within the contiguous USA. By the 1970s the command had diminished to such an extent that the decision was taken to inactivate it, and most of its assets were transferred to TAC late in 1979. TAC established 'Air Defense, Tactical Air Command' (ADTAC), a Named Unit which had the same status as a Numbered Air Force, to control these former ADC units. Unlike 9th/12th AF assets, ADTAC's assets operational role was home based; their peacetime bases were also their main wartime bases. On 6 December 1985 First Air Force (1st AF) was activated under TAC, replacing ADTAC and assuming its assets and responsibilities on that date.

Finally, a number of specialist units reported directly to TAC headquarters, rather than to one of TAC's Numbered Air Forces.

During the late 1970s and early 1980s, TAC introduced a new generation of combat aircraft. The A-7D, F-4D and F-105G left TAC service while the F-15, F-16, A-10 and secret F-117 were introduced. Also joining TAC were F-4G 'Wild Weasels', newly upgraded from F-4E airframes, while some earlier types lingered in service: F-111, RF-4C and F-4E. The F-15 and F-16 'teen fighters' would increasingly form the backbone of TAC air power, and progressively improved variants were subsequently introduced.

While space dictates that this title only covers flying units, there were (as for all USAF commands) many non-flying units throughout TAC. The majority of personnel would have served in non-flying units, such as Special Security, Civil Engineering, Air Postal, School, Computer Services, Field Printing, Management Engineering and Materiel Squadrons. Within the various wings detailed, as well as flying squadrons, supporting units included Aircraft Generation, Component Repair and Equipment Maintenance Squadrons. There was also the wing command post plus offices and units for intelligence, weapons and tactics, plans and standardisation-evaluation ('stan/eval').

By 1989 TAC had a strength of 96,406 officers and enlisted personnel, supported by 11,462 civilians, a total of 107,868. It had around 1,700 aircraft. Like other USAF commands, its flying units were organised into squadrons, generally with a 'unit establishment' of twenty-four aircraft for fighter units. Wings were typically assigned three or four squadrons.

# ADTAC/First Air Force

As outlined, TAC gained a new responsibility in 1979. Aerospace Defense Command, a USAF MAJCOM, had been responsible for providing strategic air defence forces within the contiguous USA. Remaining North American air defence forces were provided by Canadian Armed Forces and USAF Alaskan Air Command units. These forces were operationally controlled by the parallel, binational US-Canadian, North American Air Defense Command (NORAD, retitled in March 1981 with the word 'Aerospace' replacing 'Air'). ADC's commander was dual-hatted, also serving as Commander-in-Chief NORAD (CINCNORAD). ADC managed active USAF interceptor units, ground-based air defence radars and control centres, space surveillance, missile warning and related communications. ADC was responsible for day-to-day management, training, and support of these units and for providing operationally ready interceptor aircraft and aircrews (and prior to 1972 surface-to-air missiles, SAMs, too) for strategic air defence alert 24 hours per day, 365 days per year. As noted, operational control came from NORAD.

During the 1960s Soviet strategy changes saw intercontinental ballistic missiles (ICBMs) replace atomic bomb-carrying manned bombers as the primary threat to North America. Not only had the threat dramatically changed, but by the 1970s ADC's interceptor aircraft were ageing and dwindling. An increasing proportion of interceptor squadrons were assigned to the state-organised ANG rather than to ADC. The Semi-Automatic Ground Environment (SAGE) radar and command network was also ageing and requiring replacement. In size alone, ADC had withered to be no larger than a Numbered Air Force, despite being a MAJCOM.

Consequently, on 29 March 1979 the Air Force announced ADC would be inactivated as a MAJCOM and its assets distributed to three other USAF MAJCOMs. Management of active interceptor units, ground-based air defence radars and control centres would be transferred to TAC; space surveillance and missile warning resources to Strategic Air Command (SAC); and communications resources to Air Force Communications Command (AFCC). Operational control would remain with CINCNORAD.

Reorganisation, planned for the summer of 1979, was delayed by a class action lawsuit brought by ten civilian ADC employees who opposed the reorganisation, delaying reorganisation to the end of the year. On 1 October 1979 former ADC assets were transferred to TAC and AFCC, and the final ADC elements were passed to SAC on 1 December 1979. Finally, also on 1 December, the remnants of the former ADC headquarters were formed into the Aerospace Defense Center at Peterson AFB, which was a Direct Reporting Unit (reporting directly to USAF Headquarters, rather than to a USAF MAJCOM). The general commanding the Aerospace Defense Center retained the dual-hatted responsibility of also serving as CINCNORAD. Although now redundant ADC itself was not formally inactivated until 31 March 1980.

With ADC's former 'atmospheric' units (the majority of its former assets) having been passed to TAC, the latter command established 'Air Defense, Tactical Air Command' (ADTAC), a Named Unit which had the same status as a Numbered Air Force. ADTAC Headquarters was finally moved from the former ADC HQ location of Peterson AFB, Colorado, to Langley AFB in July 1981.

Former ADC assets now controlled by ADTAC were six Air Divisions for strategic air defence of the contiguous United States, plus Air Forces Iceland, the Distant Early Warning (DEW) Line and the Air Defense Weapons Center (ADWC).

## Strategic Air Defence

ADTAC's six Air Divisions were geographically organised, each controlling a Fighter Interceptor Squadron (FIS) and several Radar Squadrons within their respective areas, for administrative, training and support purposes. Each Air Division was commanded from one of the six SAGE centres ('blockhouses') and ensured that each FIS maintained round-the-clock air defence alert. As noted, NORAD had operational control of these units. Consequently, the six Air Division commanders were dual-hatted, also functioning as the NORAD Region commander for their geographic area; each Air Division acted as a NORAD Region in the parallel NORAD structure. One notable result of this arrangement was that ADTAC Air Divisions each had *administrative* control of a single regular air defence FIS unit; but when acting in their parallel NORAD Region capacity, they had *operational* control of not only that regular FIS unit, but also one or two ANG air defence FIS units within their geographic area. (Those ANG units falling under the *administrative* control of their respective states.) The ANG air defence FIS units, previously gained by ADC if federalised, were gained by TAC following the reorganisation.

The sole interceptor type in frontline ADTAC contiguous United States service at the start of the 1980s was the F-106A/F-106B Delta Dart, intended to be completely replaced by the F-15A/F-15B Eagle during the decade. However, by the end of the decade almost the entirety of the air defence mission was passed to the ANG; the final regular unit inactivated at the end of 1991. Many of these ANG squadrons also operated F-106s, while others used F-101B/F Voodoos or F-4C/F-4D Phantoms. Throughout the decade the two former ANG types would be replaced by F-15A/F-15Bs and F-16A/F-16Bs. From the very end of the decade the standard ANG F-16A/Bs were supplanted by specially modified interceptor F-16A/B ADF 'Air Defense Fighters' with added medium range air-to-air missile (AAM) capability and other features.

The F-106 (in F-106A single-seat and F-106B two-seat operational trainer versions) was the ultimate development in a series of interceptors designed for ADC. The powerful, all-weather type represented the state-of-the-art when it entered service in 1959. It could be automatically guided to its target by the SAGE system, via its advanced MA-1 fire control system. Until 1984 its armament (carried in an internal weapons bay) included the AIR-2A Genie nuclear-armed unguided air-to-air rocket. Designed to be fired into enemy bomber formations, it was armed with a 1.8Kt W-25 warhead. Various training versions were provided; the purpose-built, unarmed (apart from a spotting charge) ATR-2A, the instrumented/trackable AJT and the 'Anchor Gold' (a live AIR-2As with warhead replaced by a spotting charge). Along with a single Genie, four AIM-4F/G Super Falcon, respectively radar/infra-red (IR) guided, air-to-air missiles (AAMs) could be carried. Usually a pair of IR missiles were carried in the rear of the weapons bay and a pair of radar missiles in the front. Standard procedure was to ripple fire the two IR missiles at a single target first (in order that they did not home in on other missiles fired beforehand), followed by ripple-firing the radar missiles (either at a new target, or the original target if the IR missiles had not already destroyed it). Training Super Falcon versions were designated the Weapons System Evaluator Missile (WSEM).

Designed as a bomber-destroyer, consideration was given (later abandoned) to deploy F-106s to Vietnam. Meanwhile they were deployed to Korea during the 1968 Pueblo crisis – in either location the F-106 could have faced fighters. Furthermore it fared very well in top-secret tests against USAF-flown MiG-21s. Therefore, Project Six Shooter, launched from 1972, sought to turn the F-106 into a dog-fighter. It added G-suit compatibility, a redesigned cockpit canopy providing better visibility and an M61A1 Vulcan 20mm cannon with associated gunsight. While all F-106s received the new canopy, the gun replaced Genie capability; therefore only a minority received the gun. After Genie was retired in 1984 however, guns became more prevalent.

Replacement of F-106s with F-15A/Bs (single-/two-seater variants respectively) brought a leap in capability. However, F-15A/B service with regular air defence units was short as the mission was progressively transferred to the ANG.

The 1980 organisation was as follows. The 20th Air Division (AD) at Fort Lee Air Force Station (AFS), Virginia, covered south-east USA (up to New Jersey). It controlled the 48th FIS 'Tasmanian Devils' with the F-106A/B at Langley AFB. In its parallel capacity as the 20th NORAD Region it also had operational control over the F-106A/B equipped, Atlantic City-based, 119th FIS, 177th Fighter Interceptor Group (FIG), New Jersey ANG and the F-106A/B equipped, Jacksonville-based 159th FIS, 125th FIG, Florida ANG.

The 21st AD at Hancock Field, Syracuse, New York covered north-eastern USA (most of Pennsylvania, New Jersey, New York and the New England area plus parts of Canada) controlling the 49th FIS 'Green Eagles' with the F-106A/B at Griffiss AFB, New York. As the 21st NORAD Region it also had operational control of the Otis-based, F-106A/B equipped 101st FIS, 102d Fighter Interceptor Wing (FIW)

A pair of 48th FIS F-106A Delta Darts seen over Naval Base Charleston in 1980. (NARA)

Massachusetts ANG and the Niagara Falls-based F-101B/F equipped 136th FIS, 107th FIG New York ANG. It also had operational control of the 134th Defense Systems Evaluation Squadron (DSES), 158th Defense Systems Evaluation Group (DSEG) Vermont ANG with the EB-57B/E at Burlington; these acted as targets and Electronic Countermeasures (ECM) jammers for air defence training.

The 23d AD at Duluth International Airport, Minnesota covered a large area of the upper Midwest and parts of Canada directly to the north, controlling the 87th FIS 'Red Bulls' with the F-106A/B at K.I. Sawyer AFB, Michigan.The 87th FIS also maintained a detachment at Charleston AFB, South Carolina, under 20th NORAD Region operational control. As 23d NORAD Region it also had operational control over the F-4C equipped 171st FIS, 191st FIG, Michigan ANG at Selfridge ANGB.

The 24th AD at Malmstrom AFB, Montana roughly covered the area of the Great Plains and parts of Canada to the north, controlling the 5th FIS 'Spittin' Kittens' with the F-106A/B at Minot AFB, North Dakota. As 24th NORAD Region it also had operational control over the F-4D equipped 178th FIS, 119th FIG, North Dakota ANG at Fargo and the 186th FIS, 120th FIG Montana ANG with the F-106A/B at Great Falls.

A 49th FIS F-106A seen at Wright-Patterson AFB during 1986. The ventral bulge shows that it is carrying the M61A1 Vulcan 20mm cannon added under Project Six Shooter. It is in the standard scheme for former ADC aircraft of gloss FS 16473 'Aircraft Gray', or 'ADC Gray'. (NARA)

An air-to-air view of another 49th FIS F-106A during 1985, again featuring the ventral cannon bulge. Flying without the usual underwing drop tanks, this aircraft was possibly taking part in an air combat training sortie. (NARA)

T-33As of the 49th FIS seen during 1984. Each FIS operated a handful of T-33As for support duties, including acting as targets for interceptor training. They were modified to carry ECM and chaff pods, although none are carried here. (NARA)

This F-106A seen during 1982 belongs to the 87th FIS 'Red Bulls', featuring the prominent red bull's head tail marking of the unit. This aircraft is from the unit's detachment at Charleston AFB, South Carolina, seen in the background. (NARA)

A 5th FIS 'Spittin' Kittens' F-106A in flight during 1981; it lacks the M61A1 gun installation. (NARA)

A 5th FIS F-106A four-ship during 1981. (NARA)

5th FIS F-106As take turns refuelling from a KC-135A during 1981. From August 1967 F-106s gained air-to-air refuelling capability and supersonic drop tanks replaced the previously used subsonic ferry tanks, considerably increasing range. (NARA)

The 25th AD at McChord AFB, Washington covered north-western USA and parts of Canada to the north, controlling the 318th FIS 'Green Dragons' with the F-106A/B at McChord AFB, Washington. The unit maintained Det 1, 318th FIS with F-106s at Kingsley Field, Oregon until 30 September 1981 when Det 1 moved to Castle AFB, California (Det 1 then falling under 26th NORAD Region operational control). As the 25th NORAD Region, operational control was also exercised over the 123d FIS, 142d FIG, Oregon ANG with the F-101B/F at Portland.

Finally, the 26th AD at Luke AFB, Arizona covered south-western USA across to Texas controlling the F-106A/B equipped 84th FIS 'Black Panthers' at Castle AFB, California. As the 26th NORAD Region it also had operational control over the 111th FIS, 147th FIG Texas ANG with the F-101B/F at Ellington ANGB and 194th FIS, 144th FIW, California ANG with the F-106A/B at Fresno.

As well as their interceptors each ADTAC FIS also held a small number of T-33A trainers (modified to carry ECM and chaff pods) as targets for interceptor training. The last T-33As were withdrawn in 1988. Three of the above ADs also had a T-33 detachment for target support work; the 4787th Air Base Group (ABG) at Deluth operating T-33s on behalf of 21st AD until October 1981 and the 24th and 26th Air Defense Squadrons (ADS), respectively at Malmstrom/Luke, on behalf respectively of the 24th and 26th ADs until October 1982.

A newly received 318th FIS F-15A leads one of their retiring F-106As and a support T-33A as they transitioned between the types during September 1983. The unit's last F-106A departed McChord AFB on 2 November 1983; on 30 December the unit stood up as an operational F-15 unit. (NARA)

Support T-33As of the 318th FIS seen in flight in January 1988 immediately before their retirement ceremony. Brigadier General John M. Davey, commander, 25th Air Division, flew the lead T-33A in this formation. (NARA)

Plans were already underway prior to ADC's inactivation to replace the outdated 1950s-designed SAGE radar network. Whereas SAGE was a stand-alone, purely air defence focussed system, its replacement, the Joint Surveillance System (JSS) was jointly operated by the USAF and the Federal Aviation Administration (FAA). While SAGE was intended for peacetime and wartime use, the new JSS system was primarily intended for peacetime use; in wartime command and control could be transitioned to the new E-3A Sentry Airborne Warning and Control System (AWACS) for greater survivability.

JSS included four Regional Operations Control Centers (ROCCs) within the contiguous USA, replacing the six contiguous USA SAGE blockhouses. Consequently, ADTAC required reorganisation when JSS replaced SAGE in 1983; the six ADs (each centred on a former SAGE blockhouse) were reduced to four, one for each of the new ROCCs. The 20th and 21st ADs inactivated during 1983 (March and September respectively). The four remaining ADs were reorganised. The 23d AD moved to Tyndall AFB, Florida, and covered south-eastern USA. The 24th AD moved to Griffiss AFB,

New York, and covered north-eastern USA. The 25th AD remained at McChord AFB, Washington, and continued to cover north-western USA, although covering a wider area than before. The 26th AD moved to March AFB, California, and continued to cover the south-western USA, although with very different boundaries than before.

On 6 December 1985 First Air Force (1st AF), activated under TAC at Langley AFB, replacing and assuming the assets of ADTAC, which was inactivated.

Further reorganisation saw a reduction to two ADs and the reintroduction on 1 July 1987 of Air Defense Sectors, previously inactivated in 1966. From this date 24th AD controlled the Southeast Air Defense Sector (SEADS, Tyndall AFB) and Northeast Air Defense Sector (NEADS, Griffiss AFB, NY) while the 25th AD controlled Southwest Air Defense Sector (SWADS, March AFB, CA) and Northwest Air Defense Sector (NWADS, McChord AFB, WA). The final two ADs (24th and 25th) were inactivated on 30 September 1990, passing their remaining assets directly to their relevant Air Defense Sectors.

The development of the ADTAC/1st AF interceptor units during the decade was as follows.

The 5th FIS at Minot swapped its F-106A/Bs for F-15A/Bs during 1985. It inactivated on 1 July 1988, passing its aircraft on to the Massachusetts ANG. Unit tail-markings were a yellow lightning flash. It had transferred from 24th AD to 25th AD control on 1 June 1983, then to NWADS 1 December 1987.

The 48th FIS 'Tasmanian Devils' at Langley had been the first ADTAC unit to transition from the F-106A/B to the F-15A/B, resuming air defence alert duties with F-15s on 5 April 1982 after being stood-down for re-equipment since 4 January. On 1 July 1987 the 48th FIS finally lost its colourful squadron markings (a white chevron with blue trim and horizontal blue/white rudder stripes) and was assigned a TAC tail code of 'LY' plus blue squadron tail stripe. The only regular FIS to see out the remainder of the Cold War, it inactivated on 31 December 1991. On 1 March 1983 it transferred from 20th AD to 23d AD, briefly falling under direct 1st AF control from 1 July 1987 before reassignment to SEADS on 1 December 1987.

A pair of 48th FIS F-15As over the Wright Brothers National Memorial during 1984. (NARA)

The 49th FIS at Griffiss was inactivated on 1 July 1987; it had been the last active USAF F-106 squadron. Squadron markings were a 'fan' of white/green stripes on the rudder, later with a green eagle added at the rudder base. It transferred from 21st AD to 24th AD control on 23 September 1983.

The 84th FIS (with red/white/blue lighting strike tail-markings) at Castle became the 84th Fighter Interceptor Training Squadron (FITS) during mid-1981. Switching from the F-106A/B to the far more sedate and elderly T-33A, henceforth it specialised in electronic counter-countermeasures training plus providing targets for the weapons controller training program and various ADs. It not only provided this support to ADTAC/1st AF units, but supported TAC more widely. The unit inactivated on 27 February 1987. It remained under 26th AD control until inactivation.

The 87th FIS (with a red bull's head tail-marking) at K.I. Sawyer retained its F-106A/Bs until inactivating on 1 October 1985, having stood down from air defence alert at K.I. Sawyer on 1 February followed by its detachment at Charleston on 1 July. It transferred from 23d AD to 21st AD control on 1 August 1981, then 24th AD on 23 September 1983.

The 318th FIS at McChord became the second ADTAC unit to re-equip from F-106A/Bs to F-15A/Bs, completed on 30 December 1983. The unit lost its two-tone blue North Star unit markings and adopted a TAC-style 'TC' tail code, with two-tone blue tail-stripe, from 1 December 1987. It deactivated on 31 December 1989, maintaining its Det 1 at Castle AFB until the end. It had transferred from 25th AD to NWADS control during 1987.

Therefore by the end of the decade the strategic air defence interceptor mission had been almost entirely handed over from the active 1st AF to the ANG. Although the ANG falls outside the scope of this work, in order to complete the overview of contiguous US strategic air defence in the 1980s, a brief overview of the development of the strategic air defence ANG units mentioned above follows.

Of the five ANG units that started the 1980s with F-106A/Bs, one transitioned to the F-4D during 1984 and then to the F-16A/B ADF during 1989; one transitioned from the F-106A/B to the F-15A/B during 1988. The remaining three units transitioned from F-106A/B to F-16A/B during 1987/8 (and to F-16A/B ADF during 1990/1). Included in these latter three units was the 119th FIS, New Jersey ANG, which was the very last F-106 unit.

A pair of Det 1, 318th FIS F-15As over the Golden Gate Bridge during early 1988. The aircraft carry AIM-7 Sparrows but no AIM-9 Sidewinders, and retain full unit markings which were being phased out at this time. Det 1 operated from Castle AFB, California. (NARA)

The three ANG F-101B/F units transitioned to the F-4C during 1981/2. Two of these further transitioned to the F-4D during 1986/7 and on to the F-16A/B during 1989/90; the third unit transitioned from F-4C to the F-15A/B during 1989.

Of the two ANG FIS that started the 1980s with F-4s, one initially equipped with F-4Cs transitioned to F-4Ds during 1986 then F-16A/Bs during 1990. The other, initially equipped with F-4Ds, transitioned to F-16A/B ADFs during 1990.

Finally, two further ANG units switched role during the 1980s to join the contiguous US strategic air defence fleet, however only one of these was an operational unit. This was the 179th FIS, 148th FIG, Minnesota ANG, which had become an air defence unit and took on F-4Ds on 15 November 1983, transitioning to the F-16A/B ADF during late 1990. The final unit was the 114th TFTS, 142d TFTG, Oregon ANG; this was an ANG F-4 air defence RTU, equipped with F-4Cs from 1984. It transitioned to the F-16A/B during 1988 and the F-16A/B ADF during 1989.

## Air Forces Iceland

Responsible for the air defence of Iceland, Air Forces Iceland had been a component of ADC and transferred to ADTAC on 1 October 1979. Its sole flying unit was the 57th FIS 'Black Knights' at Naval Air Station (NAS) Keflavik in south-western Iceland. Other USAF flying units at Keflavik were not under Air Forces Iceland administration; rescue HH-3Es and their supporting HC-130N/P were provided by Military Airlift Command (MAC) as a detachment of the 67th ARRS from RAF Woodbridge, UK. Rotational deployments of a single KC-135 tanker to support the 57th FIS came from Strategic Air Command (SAC), detached from the European Tanker Task Force (ETTF), and a pair of deployed E-3s of the 960th Airborne Warning and Control Squadron (AWACS) were under direct TAC control (q.v.).

The 57th FIS operated unique main equipment compared to the contiguous US FIS units. It had re-equipped from F-4Cs to F-4Es during 1978. These were equipped with the standard AIM-7F and AIM-9E/J/P AAMs plus the internal M61A1 Vulcan 20mm cannon. However, F-4Es on alert were equipped with just four AIM-7Fs and the cannon armament, plus three external fuel tanks, but no AIM-9s. It also possessed three T-33As as training targets. Its F-4Es uniquely wore the typical ADC/ADTAC air defence grey colour scheme, unlike the tactical camouflage found on other TAC F-4Es. Squadron tail markings were a black and white checkerboard. During November 1985 the unit upgraded to F-15C/F-15Ds. Known as 'the flying tennis court' due to its large wing area, it combined outstanding manoeuvrability, long range, very capable APG-63 radar and powerful F100 engines. The F-15C/D featured various improvements over the older F-15A/B used by US-based FIS units, including increased internal fuel, plus they were able to mount Conformal Fuel Tanks (CFTs) on the fuselage sides. This feature was not generally used by USAF F-15C/Ds, however the 57th FIS fitted their jets with CFTs as standard for increased range. They were armed with the usual AIM-7M and AIM-9L/M, plus internal M61A1 cannon. The switch to F-15C/D saw the 'IS' tail code introduced, retaining their black/white checkerboard tail markings. By 1989 it operated eighteen F-15C/Ds. Eagles on alert were armed with just a pair of AIM-7Ms plus 940 rounds of 20mm ammunition for the cannon, and equipped with CFTs but no underwing or centreline external fuel tanks. The total 22,000lb of fuel carried gave around 4 hours' endurance, however the single KC-135 usually deployed supported them with air-to-air refuelling.

*Above*: F-4Es of the 57th FIS intercept an AV-MF (Soviet Naval Aviation) Tu-95RTs 'Bear-D' during 1980. 'Bears-Ds' flew very long range reconnaissance missions deep into the Atlantic. (NARA)

*Left*: As can be seen, 57th FIS alert F-4Es carried AIM-7Fs but no AIM-9s. Full ammunition was carried for the internal M61A1 cannon. (NARA)

The 57th FIS fulfilled an essential role plugging the air defence gap between European-based (primarily RAF) and North American-based (Canadian/U.S.) interceptors. Air Forces Iceland and the 57th FIS were under CINCLANT (Commander in Chief, Atlantic) operational control, rather than NORAD. They provided air defence throughout the Greenland-Iceland-UK (GIUK) gap, intercepting any unknown aircraft entering the Icelandic Military Air Defence Identification Zone (MADIZ). They maintained a pair of jets on alert at all times able to scramble at less than five minutes' notice to intercept and identify targets within the MADIZ. Conditions were tough; the nearest divert field was 700 nm away at RAF Leuchars, Scotland. Experienced pilots were selected for the unit (usually on their second tours, Captain or above). They routinely wore two layers of underwear, an anti-exposure suit and fire-retardant flying coveralls in case they ended up in the frigid waters. Pilots on standby relaxed in long johns and T-shirts, but could still don flying kit and get airborne in less than five minutes.

Typically flying sixteen sorties per day, intercepts of Soviet aircraft were commonplace – 140 per year on average. Soviet Naval Aviation (AV-MF) Tu-95/142 'Bears' were most commonly encountered, often transiting between the Kola Peninsula and Cuba. Soviet aircraft heading to Cuba were initially intercepted by Norwegian

*Above left*: A 57th FIS F-4E crew takes a close look at the 'Bear-D' tail-gunner's position. The Tu-95RTs 'Bear-D' is from the 392nd ODRAP (Independent Long-Range Reconnaissance Aviation Regiment) of the Soviet Northern Fleet based at Fedotovo, near Kipelovo, north-western USSR. (NARA)

*Above right*: F-15Cs of the 57th FIS deployed to Tyndall AFB for William Tell '88. The unit adopted the 'IS' tail code (officially 'Distinctive Unit Aircraft Identification Markings') when it re-equipped with F-15s. Here Sergeant Joe Labaska prepares AIM-9s (and below them AIM-7s) for loading during the exercise. (NARA)

fighters, RAF interceptors then escorting them through the UKADR (UK Air Defence Region) before handing off to the 57th FIS. The latter would subsequently hand-off to Canadian interceptors and then in turn USAF/ANG interceptors would provide escort down the US eastern seaboard. The routine would be reversed when the Soviet aircraft returned home. The 960th AWACS E-3s provided support; E-3s would normally scramble ahead of the fighters, following a warning from the Norwegians or NORAD (depending on direction) that Soviet aircraft were heading their way, in order to decide if a fighter scramble was required.

Also under Air Forces Iceland were two air defence General Surveillance Radar Squadrons, each operating a radar station. The 667th Aircraft Control and Warning Squadron (ACAWS) was at Hofn AS, in south-east Iceland, 230 miles east of Keflavik until inactivated on 30 September 1988. The 932d ACAWS, was at Rockville AS, in south-west Iceland, 3 miles west-northwest of Keflavik; it was redesignated 932d Air Defense Squadron on 1 October 1987. From 1987 responsibility for operating the radar stations was progressively handed from Air Forces Iceland to the Icelandic Coast Guard (in lieu of Iceland having formal armed forces) as the Iceland Air Defence System. Two new radar stations were built in north-west and north-east Iceland, joining the existing two that were upgraded. All four radar stations were handed over to Icelandic control by 1990.

## Distant Early Warning (DEW) Line

Constructed during the late 1950s, the joint US-Canadian DEW Line was a network of Arctic Circle radar stations, stretching across northern Alaska and Canada

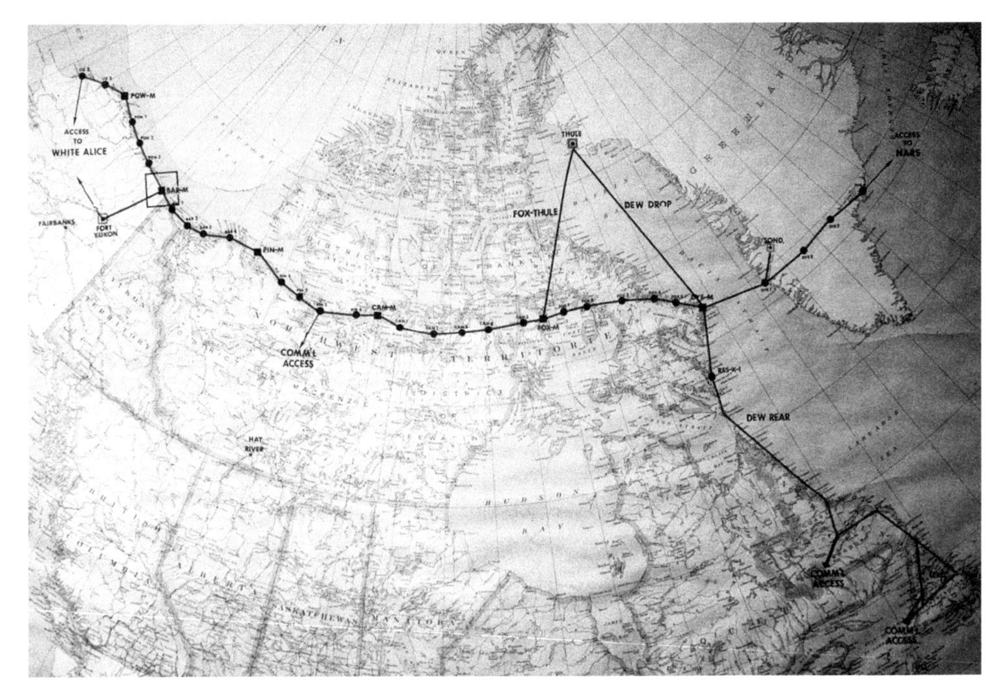


A 1980s map of DEW Line sites stretching from Alaska through Canada and into Greenland, showing the six 'Main' and twenty-seven 'Auxiliary' radar sites, plus other network elements. (NARA)

A typical DEW Line station, LIZ-2 at Point Lay, Alaska, was an AN/FPS-19 equipped 'Auxiliary' radar site. (NARA)

to Greenland. It was intended to detect hostile aircraft approaching North America over the North Pole, the most likely route for Soviet bombers. Along with other ADC assets, it became part of ADTAC on 1 October 1979.

By the early 1980s the DEW Line consisted of six 'Main' stations interspersed with twenty-seven 'Auxiliary' sites. Crews were mostly civilian contractors. Main sites had forty-five civilians plus six USAF or Canadian Armed Forces (depending on location) officers assigned. Twelve civilians made up Auxiliary site crews. Both site types featured AN/FPS-19 long-range radars, apart from the four Greenland sites with AN/FPS-30 long-range radars. All stations were remote and endured challenging Arctic conditions. Alaska was home to two Main and five Auxiliary sites,

Canada was the location of four Main and eighteen Auxiliary sites, and Greenland had four Auxiliary sites.

In 1985 the US and Canada agreed to replace the DEW Line with the updated North Warning System (NWS). From 1988, some DEW stations were deactivated and others were upgraded with new equipment, while other old, long-since deactivated, DEW sites were reactivated for NWS. NWS consisted of AN/FPS-117 equipped Long Range Radar (LRR) sites and unattended AN/FPS-124 Short Range Radar (SRR) sites. SRR sites provided 'gap-filling', looking for low-altitude targets penetrating between LRR sites. Eventually there were eleven LRR sites (four in Alaska, seven in Canada) and sixteen SRR sites (three in Alaska, thirteen in Canada). There were no NWS sites in Greenland. NWS officially replaced DEW on 15 July 1993.

## Air Defense Weapons Center (ADWC)

The ADWC at Tyndall AFB provided specialised air defence training and managed the biennial 'William Tell' air-to-air fighter meets.

In 1980 it controlled 2d FITS, 95th FITS and 475th Test Squadron (TS). All ADWC units used 'Stars and Stripes' rudder markings.

The 2d FITS operated F-106A/Bs for pilot training, plus F-101B/Fs as target tugs. While primarily an F-106 RTU, it maintained combat-ready status and could augment air defence forces in wartime if required, although it did not have an alert commitment.

The 95th FITS operated T-33As for training support (carrying ECM/chaff pods), also acting as the USAF T-33 RTU and having drone chase responsibilities.

The 475th TS provided test and evaluation support for ADWC, primarily operating F-101s and F-106s. One notable aircraft operated was the sole EF-101B, originally to be the first of eleven ECM conversions to replace EB-57s, although it was the only conversion and was later leased to Canada from October 1982.

Considerable reorganisation followed. ADWC was redesignated the 'United States Air Force Air Defense Weapons Center' on 1 March 1981 and the subordinate 325th Fighter Weapons Wing (FWW) activated on 1 July 1981. The wing had the 2d FITS, 95th FITS and 475th TS assigned, plus the newly formed 82d Tactical Aerial Target Squadron (TATS; redesignated with the word 'Targets' replacing 'Target' on 30 September 1982).

T-33A back seater's view of another 95th FITS T-33A during April 1988. By this time the 95th FITS at Tyndall AFB was the last active duty USAF T-33A unit. (NARA)

The 2d FITS passed its F-101B/F target tugs to the 82d TATS 1 July 1981 (retaining F-106A/Bs), and was redesignated 2d Fighter Weapons Squadron (FWS) on 1 February 1982 and 2d Tactical Fighter Training Squadron (TFTS) on 1 May 1984. On the latter date it transitioned to the F-15A/B, gaining 'TY' tail codes and yellow fin stripes.

On 1 January 1984 a new squadron – 1st TFTS ('TY', red tail stripe) – was assigned, bringing the first F-15A/Bs to the wing.

The 95th FITS retained its T-33As until 22 March 1988 (being the last regular USAF operator of the type), becoming the 95th TFTS on 1 April 1988 and switching to F-15A/Bs ('TY', blue tail stripe). From 1984 the 325th FWW acted as the RTU for ADTAC/1st AF, as well as ANG, F-15A/B air defence units.

The 82d TATS joined the 325th FWW on 1 July 1981, retaining the former 2d FITS F-101B/F target tugs until 1982. It also operated Full Scale Aerial Targets (FSATs) and Sub-Scale Aerial Targets (SSATs). FSATs were PQM-102A/B and QF-102A (F-102 Delta Dagger target drone conversions); SSATs were BQM-34A Firebee/BQM-34F Firebee II (subsonic/supersonic respectively) and MQM-107Bs.

The 475th TS inactivated on 15 October 1983, coinciding with the activation of the new 475th Weapons Evaluation Group (WEG) that managed range control for Gulf Range live missile firing and provided aerial targets. It gained the 82d TATS from the 325th FWW, which became the 325th Tactical Training Wing (TTW) on the same date. The 475th WEG also controlled the non-flying 81st Range Control Squadron and 83d FWS that managed the Weapon System Evaluation Program (WSEP), or 'Combat Archer'. This saw FIS/TFS units deploy to Tyndall to conduct missile firing practice against FSATs/SSATs. The 82d TATS replaced its PQM-102s/QF-102s with QF-100 FSATs during 1983. Improved MQM-107Ds joined from 1987.

Taking place on 'even' years, the biennial 'William Tell' competition was established in 1954, moving to Tyndall in 1958. Originally only open to strategic air defence units under NORAD operational control (ADC, ANG, Alaskan Air Command

An 82d TATS PQM-102B Full Scale Aerial Target approaches Tyndall AFB during 1980. Initial F-102A FSAT conversions were six QF-102As that could be flown manned or unmanned. Sixty-five PQM-102As followed, which could only be flown unmanned. Finally 146 PQM-102Bs were converted, retaining the ability to be flown manned (as pictured) or unmanned. (NARA)

An 82d TATS BQM-34F Firebee II supersonic SSAT launches at Tyndall to act as a target during William Tell '82. (NARA)

plus Canadian), from 1976 it invited competitors from TAC air-to-air units. After ADWC transferred to TAC control further changes were made. The competition's official title changed from USAF Worldwide Air-to-Air Weapons Meet to USAF Air-to-Air Weapons Meet in 1982; that year PACAF and USAFE units were invited for the first time in several years and the F-15 first participated.

William Tell 1984 saw the introduction of the QF-100 FSAT, replacing PQM-102 FSATs and BQM-34 SSATs; the first meet in which only FSATs were used as missile targets. This was also the last year that F-106 units competed (although F-106s would be involved in future years as targets and other support roles).

Competing units sent a team of five aircraft and pilots/crews, four primary and one spare. Phases of the competition, known as 'Profiles', made use of an Air Combat Manoeuvring Instrumentation (ACMI) range, firing internal cannons at towed targets and firing live AAMs (with warheads replaced by telemetry packages) at aerial targets. Profiles I and II were flown on a single mission, as a two-ship from each team. Profile I was a frontal radar missile attack against a QF-100 FSAT, Profile II seeing the same target attacked from the rear by IR missiles. Profile III tested the team's ability to scramble, identify and engage two manned targets with two interceptors; both carried two each 'captive' (non-firing) IR and radar missiles. Each target had to be 'killed' by an IR and radar missile; one interceptor could 'kill' both targets if necessary. Profile IV saw each team launch all four aircraft to intercept a massed raid of manned targets at various altitudes/speeds, a typical example consisting of three F-111s, two B-52s, two ECM T-33s and two F-106s simulating cruise missiles. Each team aircraft was equipped with three simulated missiles. Twelve targets were to be engaged (target aircraft made multiple passes through the exercise area to provide sufficient targets). All simulated missile shots had to be on target to obtain maximum points.

*Above left*: An 82d TATS QF-100D FSAT during William Tell '86. The wingtip Continuous Infrared Radiation (CIR) pods were intended to draw AIM-9 Sidewinders towards the wingtips rather than the engine; even Sidewinders without warheads (as fired at the FSATs) could easily bring one down if the engine/fuselage was hit. These telemetered pods dramatically increased the lifespan of the QF-100s while providing kill data for the missiles launched at the FSAT. (NARA)

*Above right*: Contractor Dick McKibben controls a QF-100 FSAT while colleague Gordy Pollard looks on during William Tell '86. (NARA)

Profile V (introduced solely for attending Active Duty units in 1984 and extended to ANG units from 1986 after they introduced 20mm gun pods for their F-4s), involved live fire aerial gunnery against towed targets (initially towed by F-4s, in later years by F-15s). Each participant was limited to 150 rounds.

Collated Profile scores determined the awards. There were 'Top Team' and 'Category Best Team' awards, Category I being F-15 (and Canadian CF-18), Category II being F-4 and Category III being F-106. Individual aircrew scores determined the overall 'Top Gun' pilot/crew, as well as Category 'Top Guns'. There were also awards for ground support personnel and awards from various involved defence contractors. Finally the 'Top Aerial Gunner' and 'Top Aerial Gunnery Team' awards went to the Profile V winners.

Copper Flag was a realistic, ADWC-managed, air defence/defensive counter-air exercise over the Gulf of Mexico. Held from April 1982, it was conducted three times a year. Four fighter units took part in the two-week exercise as the 'Blue Force' alongside E-3s. Units usually brought six aircraft and nine aircrews, switching the deployed aircrew at the end of the first week so that a total of eighteen unit crews participated. The opposing 'Red Force' came from other USAF units (e.g. B-52s, EF/FB/F-111s, RF-4Cs, T-33s and F-106s) often supported by Canadian EF-101B/CC-117 Falcon ECM trainers and USN aircraft. Unlike other large exercises it continued at night and in instrument/weather conditions. Blue Force fighters contended with heavy ECM, communications jamming and chaff while intercepting diverse threats. In a typical sortie they might have faced an F-111 at Mach 2.0 and 40,000 feet, an RF-4C at low-level at 500 knots and T-33s/F-106s simulating cruise missiles.

# Ninth Air Force

Ninth Air Force (9th AF, headquarters Shaw AFB, South Carolina) held TAC's assets in the eastern contiguous USA.

The 1st TFW ('FF' tail code) at Langley AFB controlled the 27th Tactical Fighter Squadron (TFS) 'Eagles' (yellow tail stripe), 71st TFS 'Ironmen' (red) and the 94th TFS 'Spads'/'Hat in the Ring' (blue). It upgraded from F-15A/B to F-15C/D models during 1981–1982. The F-15 was designed as a pure air superiority/interceptor type and envisaged as having 'not a pound for air-to-ground'. However, due to their RDJTF commitments, the 1st TFW unusually employed the F-15C/D's secondary air-to-ground capability, possessing Multiple Ejector Racks (MERs) from which Mk 82/84 dumb bombs or cluster bomb units (CBUs) could be hung. The 1st TFW even attended a mid-1980s Red Flag exercise as the host air-to-ground unit, for which they had gone to the effort of adding temporary removable stripes of brown camouflage paint to the upper surfaces of their F-15s. Predictably this caused some good natured jibes from other unit's pilots, who mockingly referred to their mounts as 'B-15 Beagles'! The 1st TFW also had a supply of CFTs for their F-15C/Ds. When the F-15C/D later went through the Multi-Stage Improvement Program (MSIP) upgrades (with improved radars, avionics and other systems) their secondary air-to-ground capabilities were lost; the wing's MERs and CFTs were sold to Saudi Arabia. Questions remained about wartime air-to-air rules of engagement (ROE), especially for units deployed to Europe. The crowded skies expected would probably dictate visual identification (VID) of targets, precluding medium range AIM-7M use. Even if it could be used, AIM-7 was limited in requiring the launching aircraft to fly towards the target, maintaining radar contact until missile impact. Consequently, the replacement 'fire-and-forget' AIM-120 AMRAAM (Advanced Medium Range AAM) was developed, but protracted development meant that the AIM-7 would see out the remainder of the Cold War. On 7 August 1983, due to the Libyan intervention in Chad and in accordance with its RDJTF commitments, 94th TFS deployed eight F-15Cs and sixteen pilots to Khartoum, Sudan (along with two E-3As and two SAC KC-10As) for twenty days. Also under 1st TFW control was the 6th Airborne Command and Control Squadron (ACCS) with the EC-135P (no tail code). These supported U.S. Commander in Chief, Atlantic Command (USCINCLANT), deploying throughout the Atlantic region. The wing HQ also had a handful of UH-1P helicopters for support work until 1987 when the 4401st Helicopter Flight was created and UH-1Ns replaced the old UH-1Ps.

The 4th TFW ('SJ') at Seymour Johnson AFB, North Carolina controlled the 334th TFS 'Eagles' (blue), 335th TFS 'Chiefs' (green) and 336th TFS 'Rocketeers' (yellow) with F-4Es upgraded with the much improved ARN-101 digital nav-attack system. It also briefly operated a fourth squadron from 1 April 1982 to 1 July 1985,

F-15Cs of the 1st TFW over Fort Monroe during 1983, each in unit commander's markings, from nearest 94th TFS, 71st TFS, 1st TFW and 27th TFS. (NARA)

Five 1st TFW F-15Cs shutting down after arrival at Tyndall AFB to compete in William Tell '84. As can be seen on the background F-15C's tail, the 1st TFW's William Tell team aircraft had the usual squadron tail colours replaced with yellow/red/blue stripes, representing each squadron in the wing. The 1st TFW William Tell '84 team ultimately came in fourth place; first through third places went respectively to the 33rd TFW (F-15C), 49th TFW (F-15A) and 142nd FIG, Oregon ANG (F-4C). (NARA)

A 71st TFS F-15C at Wright-Patterson AFB during 1987. (NARA)

A 4th TFW F-4E competing in Gunsmoke '81, about to drop BDU-33 25-pound practice 'blue bombs' on target over the Nellis ranges. Gunsmoke, officially the USAF Worldwide Gunnery Meet, was held at Nellis AFB biennially in 'odd' years, alternating with William Tell which was held in 'even' years. It was the USAF's premier conventional air-to-surface bombing competition. This F-4E features toned-down markings and the wraparound version of the South East Asia (SEA) camouflage scheme; camouflage colours extended to the undersides, covering formerly light grey undersides. For Gunsmoke '81 the 4th TFW team's F-4Es received red tail stripes, replacing individual squadron (blue, green or yellow) stripes. The following year the 337th TFS was assigned to the 4th TFW and adopted the red trail stripe as its squadron colour. (NARA)

Twelve F-4Es of the 335th TFS, 4th TFW made the ‘Coronet Musket’ deployment to Karup AB, Denmark from 12 August to 2 September 1982. Here seven of their F-4Es are seen on the Karup flightline. (NARA)

A 335th TFS, 4th TFW F-4E returning to Karup after a ‘Coronet Musket’ mission. The fairing on the spine is the main recognition feature of the AN/ARN-101 Digital Modular Avionics System (DMAS). This was retrofitted to many F-4Es/F-4Gs/RF-4Cs, including all 4th TFW F-4Es, apart from those of the 337th TFS during its brief existence. ARN-101, known as ‘Arnie’ to crews, replaced analogue systems with integrated digital ones, giving much improved navigation and air-to-ground accuracy while easing the crew’s burden. (NARA)

A 4th TFW F-4E during air defence exercise Amalgam Chief '88. The F-4 variant of 'European I' wraparound camouflage had been adopted mid-decade; this retained the dark green (FS 34079) and medium green (FS 34102) used in the 'SEA' scheme, but replaced the former dark tan (FS 30219) with dark grey (FS 36081). A-10s had also adopted 'European I' but the F-4 variant substituted FS 34079 dark green for the A-10's FS 34092 dark green. The ASX-1 TISEO pod on the left wing leading edge, introduced in late production F-4Es, was an electro optical system intended to identify air-to-air targets beyond visual range. Ultimately it saw greater use identifying navigational way points during air-to-ground use. A 'deep' ALQ-131 ECM pod is also carried. (NARA)

the 337th TFS 'Falcons' (red), the latter adopting ex-21st TFW (Elmendorf AFB, Alaska) F-4Es that lacked ARN-101. The 4th TFW started converting to the new F-15E when 336th TFS re-equipped during 1989; the remaining squadrons followed in 1990/1. Developed from the air superiority Eagle, the two-seat (pilot and dedicated Weapons Systems Operator) F-15E Strike Eagle was intended for strike/interdiction, while retaining the Eagle's deadly air-to-air capability. Featuring upgraded avionics, including AN/APG-70 radar and the LANTIRN (Low-Altitude Navigation and Targeting Infra-Red for Night) system in two underside pods. These were the AN/AAQ-13 navigation pod (to starboard) with a terrain-following radar (TFR) and forward looking infrared (FLIR) camera, the image of which projected onto the wide field-of-view heads up display (HUD), and the AN/AAQ-14 targeting pod (to port) with an articulated head mounting a FLIR with boresighted laser designator. AN/AAQ-14 was used to guide Laser Guided Bombs (LGBs) and hand-off targets to AGM-65D/G Maverick IR missiles. LANTIRN was originally intended to give A-10s and F-16s night attack capabilities; the F-15E actually became the system's launch type, closely followed by F-16s, the A-10 being dropped from the programme. AN/AAQ-13 deliveries started in 1987. However, AN/AAQ-14 initially proved problematic – deliveries started in 1988 and were slow. Even by the time of the 1991 Gulf War, there were only enough AN/AAQ-14 pods available to equip a handful of F-15Es (and none for F-16Cs). As well as LGBs and Mavericks, F-15E ordnance included CBUs, Mk 82/84 dumb bombs, GBU-15 glide bombs and B61 tactical nuclear bombs, plus all the usual F-15 air-to-air weapons. Although its large wings gave a bumpier low-level ride than a dedicated striker like the F-111, they also bestowed manoeuvrability – advantageous if bounced by enemy interceptors. F-111 crews (who relied purely on speed to evade enemy aircraft) could only dream of such manoeuvrability.

The 23d TFW ('EL') at England AFB, Louisiana was TAC's last frontline A-7D unit. Assigned the 74th TFS 'Flying Tigers' (blue), 75th TFS 'Tiger Sharks' (black/white) and 76th TFS 'Vanguards' (red). The squadrons re-equipped with the A-10A during March, the summer and October 1981 respectively. During Operation Urgent Fury,

A newly received 336th TFS, 4th TFW F-15Es seen in 1989. The aircraft is only carrying the LANTIRN AN/AAQ-13 navigation pod; the delayed AN/AAQ-14 targeting pods were absent for an extended period after the F-15E's introduction. It also carries a CATM-9L/M (AIM-9L/M Sidewinder captive training round) and inert Mk 82 500lb Low Drag General Purpose (LDGP) training bombs. (NARA)

A KC-10A boom operator's view of the same 336th TFS F-15E seen in the previous image. The presence of AN/AAQ-13 but lack of AN/AAQ-14 is clearly visible, along with the training Mk 82s and CATM-9L/M. It is in the standard F-15E overall FS 36118 'Dark Gray' camouflage. (NARA)

A 76th TFS, 23d TFW A-7D dropping live Mk 82 'Snakeye' retarded 500lb bombs over Claiborne Range, Louisiana during 1980, the last full year of 23d TFW A-7D operations. It features wraparound SEA camouflage and the wing's distinctive 'shark's mouth' markings, inherited from their Second World War American Volunteer Group forebears. (NARA)

A 23d TFW A-10A at Nellis AFB participating in Gunsmoke '81. The A-10 'European I' scheme, adopted after A-10s were initially delivered in light grey, consisted of lustreless FS 36081 'Dark Gray', FS 34102 'Light Green' and FS 34092 'Dark Green'. (NARA)

the October–November 1983 US invasion of Grenada, 76th TFS deployed to Roosevelt Roads Naval Station, Puerto Rico, to fly supporting missions.

The A-10A Thunderbolt was a revolutionary, survivable, tank-killing and CAS (close air support) type designed around its massive GAU-8/A Avenger, seven-barrelled, 30mm cannon. Firing sixty-five depleted uranium shells per second, the standard 'combat mix' of ammunition (for anti-armour) was a five-to-one mix of PGU-14/B Armor Piercing Incendiary (API) and PGU-13/B High Explosive Incendiary (HEI) rounds. The A-10 was flyable even if one engine, one tail section or a large wing section was shot off and featured triple-redundant flight controls with control cables (less susceptible to jamming if damaged) rather than rods. Its eleven hardpoints could carry a considerable war load. The AGM-65 Maverick air-to-ground missile was the primary anti-tank weapon, early daytime-only (TV seeker head) AGM-65A and B models being joined by imaging infra-red (IIR) AGM-65Ds from 1986. AGM-65G with IIR plus heavyweight penetrator warhead entered service late in the decade. CBUs were available for area targets, including new CBU-87/89 or older Mk 20 Rockeye and SUU-30H dispenser family models. Mk 82s were also an option. Self-defence AIM-9L/Ms were carried as well as ECM pods. The 'AirLand Battle' concept, adopted in 1982, emphasised a 'joint' (combined Army/Air Force) approach, also focussing on exploiting US technological advantages, especially night fighting where US forces had an advantage. The importance of striking 'follow-on forces' deeper behind the frontline, isolating frontline enemy forces from reinforcements, was also stressed. Some within the USAF leadership were hostile to the Army-supporting CAS mission in general and the A-10 specifically. This hostility and the new 'AirLand Battle' vision resulted in the USAF's new Close Air Support/Battlefield Air Interdiction (CAS/BAI) requirement. This was for an A-10 replacement, with A-10 relegated to the 'Fast-FAC' (forward air controller) role (replacing OA-37B and OV-10A). Options explored for the new CAS/BAI type included a dedicated CAS F-16 variant (known for a time as the 'A-16 Block 60') and the A-7F (a rebuilt supersonic night/adverse weather version of the A-7D). From 1987 the USAF did start to re-role a small number of A-10As for FAC (redesignated OA-10A despite being unmodified) while New York ANG F-16As adopted the CAS role, adding a 30mm podded gun (GPU-5). However Congress intervened in 1990, ordering the USAF to retain two A-10 wings. The 'A-16' (and successor 'F/A-16' proposal) were not adopted and the A-7F did not proceed beyond a pair of YA-7F prototypes; the A-10 survived as the USAF's premier CAS type for several more decades.

A-10A pilots of the 23d TFW Gunsmoke '81 team prepare for another mission from Nellis AFB. Gunsmoke '81 was the first since 1964, the Vietnam War causing the seventeen year hiatus. Gunsmoke '81 involved A-7, A-10 and F-4 teams; Gunsmoke '83 saw F-16 teams join, which dominated in subsequent years. Gunsmoke involved three 'Profiles'; Profiles I and II saw various four-ship team missions involving level, dive and 'pop up' attacks with BDU-33 25-pound practice 'blue bombs', plus strafing. Profile III, was considered the most difficult, where the competition was won or lost. It involved two-ship missions, navigating along a 150–200 mile course then dropping inert 500lb practice bombs fitted with Air Inflatable Retarders on a specific target within a large simulated airfield complex. Competition judges also scrutinised weapons load crews with scored integrated combat turnaround (ICT) 'Loadeo' loading contests. (NARA)

A 23d TFW A-10A during Gunsmoke '81. Similarly to air-to-air wings attending William Tell, air-to-ground wings attending Gunsmoke sent five aircraft (four primary plus a spare), and drew airframes from across their wing. Consequently, each team used special markings in place of the usual squadron markings. As seen, the 23d TFW's team adopted fin markings combining the colours of all three squadrons assigned to the wing. Gunsmoke was open to teams from across the Tactical Air Forces – TAC, USAFE, PACAF, ANG and Air Force Reserve. (NARA)

The 31st TFW ('ZF', replaced by 'HS' 1 December 1986) at Homestead AFB, Florida was redesignated 31st TTW on 30 March 1981, reverting to 31st TFW on 1 October 1985. At the start of the decade its squadrons were in the process of converting from combat-coded F-4E units to F-4D equipped RTUs, later reverting to combat-ready status with the F-16A/B. The 306th TFTS 'Gunners' (yellow) with F-4Ds inactivated on 1 September 1983, reactivating on 1 October 1985 with F-16A/Bs as the 306th TFS. It inactivated again on 31 October 1986, passing its personnel and equipment to the 308th TFS the next day (q.v.). The 307th TFS 'Stingers' (red) converted from F-4Es to F-4Ds during 1980 becoming 307th TFTS on 1 July 1983. It converted to the F-16A/B, becoming the 307th TFS once again on 1 April 1988, inactivating on 1 July 1989. The 308th TFS 'Emerald Knights' (green) converted from F-4Es to F-4Ds, becoming 308th TFTS on 9 October 1980. Taking over former 306th TFS personnel and equipment on 1 November 1986, it became 308th TFS with F-16A/B. Finally the 309th TFS 'Wild Ducks' (blue) converted from F-4Es to F-4Ds during 1980 becoming 309th TFTS on 1 July 1982. On 1 October 1986, it converted to the F-16A/B and became the 309th TFS.

The multi-role F-16A/B (respectively single-/two-seat) variants, delivered to the USAF from January 1979, were produced in a series of 'Block' sub-types. The initial F-16A/B Block 1 featured a black radome (which proved too conspicuous in air-to-air combat), a UHF blade antenna under the intake and F100-PW-200 turbofan. They were quickly superseded by Block 5, introducing a grey radome. Block 10 introduced minor internal changes; all Block 1 and 5 aircraft were subsequently upgraded to this standard. The definitive F-16A/B was Block 15. This introduced side-by-side hardpoints under the intake (although these were not utilised by the USAF until the later F-16C/F-16D variants). To offset these a 'big tail' (30 percent larger

*Above*: A 307th TFTS, 31st TFW F-4D sits behind munitions specialists preparing AIM-9P-3 and AIM-7E AAMs at Homestead AFB during Exercise Solid Shield '87. (NARA)

*Left*: A 307th TFTS, 31st TFW F-4D launches from MacDill AFB in 1987 while taking part in Long Rifle III, a semi-annual air-to-ground gunnery competition. An SUU-23 20mm gun pod is carried on the centreline. (NARA)

horizontal stabiliser) was introduced. This also reduced take-off rotation angle and allowed stable flight at higher angles of attack. Block 15 replaced the under-intake blade antenna by a pair of side-by-side under-nose antennas, introduced rudimentary 'track-while-scan' capability to the AN/APG-66 radar, along with Have Quick I secure UHF radios, rearranged cockpit instruments, and airframe strengthening allowing heavier under-wing loads. Some Block 15s were later modified to the Air Defense Fighter (ADF) configuration for ANG FIS units as outlined previously. TAC used the F-16 primarily in the air-to-ground role, with air-to-air as secondary. Typical period F-16A/B ordnance included Mk 82/84 slick or retarded bombs, CBUs, AGM-65A/Bs and B61 tactical nuclear bombs, as well as AIM-9P/L/M short-range AAMs.

The 33d TFW ('EG') at Eglin AFB, Florida converted from F-4Es to F-15A/Bs during 1978/9, controlling the 58th TFS 'Gorillas' (blue), 59th TFS 'Golden Pride' (yellow) and 60th TFS 'Crows' (red). On 3 July 1979 the 33d TFW received the first F-15C

A 306th TFS, 31st TFW F-16A Block 15 at Homestead ABF during 1986, shortly before the wing changed from 'ZF' tail codes to 'HS'. (NARA)

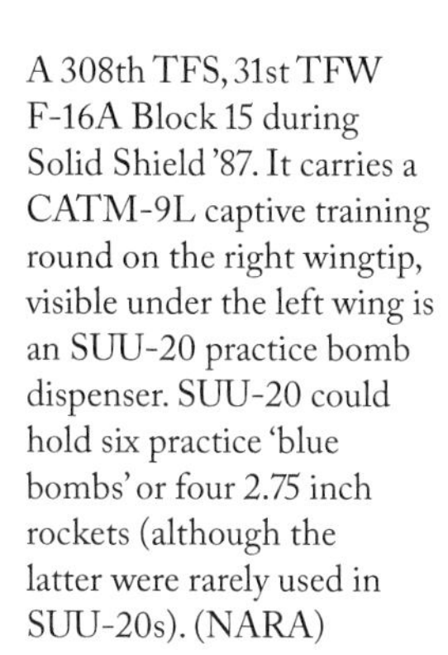

A 308th TFS, 31st TFW F-16A Block 15 during Solid Shield '87. It carries a CATM-9L captive training round on the right wingtip, visible under the left wing is an SUU-20 practice bomb dispenser. SUU-20 could hold six practice 'blue bombs' or four 2.75 inch rockets (although the latter were rarely used in SUU-20s). (NARA)

delivered to an operation unit, passing its F-15A/Bs to the 49th TFW at Holloman by early 1980. During 1979/80 33d TFW supported the re-equipment of PACAF's 18th TFW (based at Kadena, Okinawa), training fifty-five pilots, also transferring fifty-four F-15C/Ds to the latter wing under 'Ready Eagle III'. The 33d TFW reverted to F-15A/Bs from 5 June 1980, receiving ex-USAFE 36th TFW (Bitburg) airframes. From 1983, the wing transitioned again to F-15C/Ds; during 1987–1989 the wing converted to upgraded F-15C/D MSIP variants. Eight 33d TFW F-15s provided air cover during Operation Urgent Fury over Grenada in 1983, preventing interference by Cuban aircraft. It also provided air cover for Operation Just Cause, the December 1989–January 1990 US intervention in Panama.

The 56th TFW ('MC') at MacDill AFB, Florida became the 56th TTW on 1 October 1981 and was transitioning its squadrons from combat-coded F-4D units to RTU F-16A/B units, as follows: The 13th TFTS (black) with F-4Ds inactivated on 1 July 1982. The 61st TFTS 'Top Dogs' (yellow) transitioned to the F-16A/B on 1 January 1980 (previously being the 61st TFS with F-4Ds). It re-equipped with F-16C/D Block 30s from autumn 1988, completed by 28 June 1989. The 62d TFS 'Spikes' (blue) with

F-15As of the 58th TFS, 33d TFW crossing the Florida coast during Exercise Ocean Venture '82, carrying CATM-9Ls and centreline 600 US gal tanks. (NARA)

A 60th TFS, 33d TFW F-15C deployed to Canadian Forces Base Lahr, West Germany during 'Coronet Phaser'. Held 24 September to 20 October 1987, Coronet Phaser involved around twenty-four F-15C/Ds of both the 58th TFS and 60th TFS of the 33rd TFW deploying to Lahr from Eglin AFB, Florida. This F-15C carries a captive training Sidewinder and centreline 600 US gal tank. (NARA)

*Above*: Four 58th TFS, 33d TFW F-15Cs over the West German countryside during Coronet Phaser. All carry centreline 600 US gal tanks. The three furthest aircraft each have captive training sidewinders on the inboard shoulder rails under the right wing; the nearest Eagle presumably carries one on the other side. (NARA)

*Right*: The rear seat view from a 33d TFW F-15D of another Eagle during Coronet Phaser in West Germany. (NARA)

A 58th TFS F-15C, deployed to Tyndall AFB, launches an AIM-7 Sparrow at a FSAT/SSAT over the Gulf Range during Combat Archer, the Weapon System Evaluation Program, in 1988. Combat Archer allowed units to conduct missile firing practice. (NARA)

*Left*: A 59th TFS, 33d TFW F-15C shows off its load of early captive training versions of the AIM-120 AMRAAM, along with captive CATM-9L/Ms and centreline tank, during 1989. (NARA)

*Below*: The same AMRAAM and Sidewinder-toting 59th TFS F-15C seen in the previous image, flies along the Florida coast as it returns to Eglin AFB. It is in the then-standard F-15 'Ghost Gray' camouflage scheme of FS 36375 'Light Gray' and FS 36320 'Dark Gray'. (NARA)

the F-4D became the 62d TFTS with F-16A/Bs from 1 January 1981, re-equipping with F-16C/D Block 30s by 27 June 1989. The 63d TFS 'Panthers' (red) with F-4Ds became 63d TFTS with F-16A/B from 1 October 1981, re-equipping with F-16C/D Block 30s by 31 July 1989. From 1 July 1982 the 72d TFTS 'Falcons' (black), with the F-16A/B, was assigned replacing the 13th TFTS which had inactivated the same day. The 72d re-equipped with F-16C/D Block 25/30 from March 1990. The wing also had 'MC' coded UH-1Ps directly assigned from 1978–1987.

The 347th TFW ('MY') at Moody AFB, Georgia operated the F-4E, assigned the 68th TFS 'Lightning Lancers' (red), 70th TFS 'White Knights' (blue/white) and 339th TFS 'Dragons' (Silver). The 339th inactivated on 1 July 1983, replaced the same day by the 69th TFS 'Werewolves' (silver) which took over the 339th's aircraft and crews. The wing re-equipped with F-16A/B Block 15s during 1987–1988 (the 68th by 1 April 1987, 70th by 1 October 1987 and the 69th by 1 January 1988).

A 61st TFTS, 56th TTW F-16A Block 10 during 1987. It is in the standard F-16 'Egyptian I' scheme of FS 36270 'Medium Gray'/FS 36118 'Dark Gray' upper-sides with FS 36375 'Light Gray' undersides. (NARA)

A 347th TFW F-4E in 1980. It carries six Mk 82 bombs on a centreline Multiple Ejector Rack (MER), a port inboard 2,000-pound GBU-10 Paveway II LGB, an AVQ-23 Pave Spike laser designator pod, two starboard inboard AIM-9Js and a pair of 370 US gal external fuel tanks. Unlike later systems Pave Spike used TV optics, rather than IR, limiting its use to daylight visual conditions. (NARA)

The 347th TFW F-4E seen in the previous image 'pickles' its load of six Mk 82 LDGP bombs over a bombing range in Florida. It carries 347th TFW wing commander's markings and is in SEA camouflage of FS 34102 'Medium Green', FS 34079 'Dark Green' and FS 30219 'Dark Tan' upper sides with FS 36622 'Light Gray' undersides. (NARA)

A 68th TFS, 347th TFW F-4E is seen in formation with an Egyptian 222nd TFB F-4E during Exercise Proud Phantom in 1980, the first USAF tactical deployment to Egypt. The 347th TFW deployed twelve F-4Es to Cairo West AB from July to October. The Egyptian Air Force (EAF), hitherto equipped with Soviet types, was struggling with their recently received ex-USAF (former 31st TFW) F-4Es. Therefore the 347th TFW helped the EAF's 222nd TFB's (Wing's) 76th and 88th Squadrons build up serviceability. Success was limited; Egyptian serviceability only reached 45 to 50 percent by Proud Phantom's conclusion. Egypt decided to retain their F-4Es, having contemplated selling them to Turkey, after a US Technical Assistance Field Team finally got serviceability to 80 percent by mid-1983. (NARA)

A pair of 70th TFS, 347th TFW, F-4Es take turns refuelling from a KC-135A (of the 19th Air Refueling Wing, Heavy from Robins AFB, Georgia) during Exercise Gallant Eagle '84. The nearest F-4E carries Pave Spike. (NARA)

A 70th TFS, 347th TFW, F-4E participating in the Copper Flag air defence/defensive counter-air exercise over the Gulf of Mexico. The aircraft carries 370 US gal underwing and 600 US gal centreline fuel tanks, plus an AN/ALQ-119 ECM pod. Out of view is a CATM-9P Sidewinder training round. The unit reequipped with F-16A/B Block 15s a short time later. (NARA)

The A-10A-equipped 354th TFW ('MB') at Myrtle Beach AFB, South Carolina, controlled the 353d TFS 'Panthers' (red), the 355th TFS 'White Falcons' (white with blue stars, solid blue from 1984) and the 356th TFS 'Green Demons' (green). During November 1979 the 363d TFS undertook the Coronet Loop deployment to Guantanamo, Cuba, demonstrating American displeasure at the presence of a Soviet brigade on the island.

The 363d Tactical Reconnaissance Wing (TRW) ('JO', replaced by 'SW' from 1 April 1982) with RF-4Cs at Shaw AFB, South Carolina became the 363d TFW on 1 October 1982 switching from a reconnaissance RTU to mixed fighter (F-16) and reconnaissance duties. (RF-4C training moved to the 67th TRW at Bergstrom during 1982.) The 363d's 16th TRS (red/yellow/black/white) retained RF-4Cs, switched to 'SW' codes from 1 July 1982 and inactivated on 15 December 1989. The 33d TRTS 'Claws' (blue) with RF-4Cs inactivated 1 October 1982 retaining the 'JO' codes to the end. It reactivated 1 January 1985 as the 33d TFS 'Falcons' (blue) with F-16C/D Block 25, transitioning to Block 42s during 1991. The 62d TRS (red) with RF-4Cs was reassigned to the 67th TRW (q.v.) as the 62d TRTS on 1 July 1982. On 1 April 1982 the 19th TFS 'Gamecocks' (yellow) was activated with F-16A/B Block 10s, transitioning to Block 15s during 1984, F-16C/D Block 25s during summer 1985 and Block 42s during 1991. On 1 July 1982 the 17th TFS 'Hooters' (white) activated with F-16A/B Block 10s, re-equipped with Block 15s during 1984, F-16C/D Block 25 from autumn 1985 and Block 42s during 1991.

A four-ship of 353d TFS, 354th TFW, A-10As while deployed to Eielson AFB for Exercise Brim Frost '81 in Alaska. (NARA)

*Above left*: A 353d TFS, 354th TFW, A-10A arrives at Leck AB, West Germany for Crested Cap (Autumn Forge) in 1982. The 353d TFS deployed twelve A-10As to Leck from 26 August to 27 September 1982. Crested Cap was the USAF counterpart to the US Army's 'REFORGER' (Return of Forces to Germany) exercise. The 600 US gal ferry tank used by the A-10, here being removed, was the same type used by the F-111. (NARA)

*Above right*: A-10As of the 355th TFS, 354th TFW, during Thunderhog V in 1983 at Myrtle Beach AFB. The wing used a wooded area of their base for the annual Thunderhog exercise, simulating operations from austere European forward operating locations. (NARA)

A 62d TRS, 363d TRW, RF-4C over Florida during a training mission in 1980. This RF-4C features SEA camouflage and full-colour national star insignia. (NARA)

A 62d TRS, 363d TRW, RF-4C with wraparound SEA camouflage with toned-down national star insignia, while deployed to RAF Alconbury for Salty Bee '82. The 62d TRS deployed eighteen RF-4Cs for this exercise between 20 May and 23 June 1982. On 1 July 1982, just a week after returning home, 62d TRS was transferred to the 67th TRW at Bergstrom AFB, Texas, as 62d TRTS. (NARA)

A 19th TFS, 363d TFW F-16A Block 15 deployed to George AFB for Exercise Air Warrior in 1984. An MJ-1 'Jammer' lift truck is about to load a TGM-65B CATM (inert captive training AGM-65B Maverick variant). The TGM-65B is mounted on an LAU-88/A triple-rail missile launcher. (NARA)

More 19th TFS, 363d TFW F-16As during Air Warrior in 1984 during a training mission over Fort Irwin. While the aircraft in the previous image was a Block 15, these are earlier Block 10s. Their left-side LAU-88/A Maverick launchers are empty, however a training Maverick is under the nearest jet's right wing, its fins just visible protruding below the centreline tank. The nearest aircraft has a CATM-9L on the port wingtip, while the distant aircraft carries in the same position an Acceleration Monitor Assembly (AMA) pod. The latter is a radar reflector used for training purposes. Both carry 300 US gal centreline fuel tanks. (NARA)

A 33d TFS, 363d TFW F-16C Block 25, in squadron commander's markings, leading a Royal Jordanian Air Force F-5F during Exercise Shadow Hawk '87 in Jordan, a phase of Bright Star '87. The F-16C carries a CATM-9L and an AMA pod, while the Jordanian F-5F carries a CATM-9P. (NARA)

The F-16C/D (single-/two-seat) variants featured a larger vertical fin base than F-16A/Bs; intended to house an internal ECM system, this was later abandoned leaving F-16C/Ds still reliant on external ECM pods. The initial F-16C/D Block 25 introduced new AN/APG-68 radar, wide angle HUD and added AGM-65D Maverick (IR) compatibility among other improvements. It retained the F100-PW-200, although Block 25 aircraft were later retrofitted with more reliable F100-PW-220 or F100-PW-220E engines (F100-PW-220s were new build engines, while F100-PW-220Es were -200s modified to -220 configuration). To drive down costs the Alternative Fighter Engine (AFE) program was initiated in 1984, introducing the General Electric F110 as an alternative to the Pratt & Whitney F100 from the

Block 30/32 onwards. Block 30 utilised the F110-GE-100; after initially retaining the standard intake, later Block 30 production introduced an enlarged 'big mouth' intake catering for the larger air-flow mass required by the F110-GE-100. Block 32 retained the F100-PW-220. Block 30/32 introduced AGM-45 Shrike, AGM-88 HARM and AIM-120 compatibility. Generally USAF policy was to assign GE-powered Block 30s to overseas (PACAF and USAFE) units and P&W-powered Block 32 aircraft to US-based (TAC) units. The final 1980s era F-16C/D sub-types were the Block 40/42 'Night Falcons', which offered the same engine options as Block 30/32. Entering service from December 1988, these introduced LANTIRN, providing night low-level flight and precision attack capabilities. Block 40/42s carried AN/AAQ-13 to port and AN/AAQ-14 to starboard, the reverse of how F-15Es carried them. Delays with the targeting pod meant that initially only navigation pods were used. Other Block 40/42 upgrades included modified undercarriage, strengthened structure (allowing operation at higher weights), updated radar and an even larger HUD. Digital flight controls replaced analogue ones, allowing the AN/AAQ-13 navigation pod to directly operate the controls for automatic terrain following flight.

The 507th Tactical Air Control Wing (TAIRCW) at Shaw AFB ('VA', until 1984/5 when 'SR' was adopted), was not primarily a flying wing, being concerned with managing the 'Tactical Air Control System' of mobile ground-based radars, Tactical Air Control Parties (TACPs) etc. However, it also included supporting flying units with fixed wing observation/FAC aircraft plus helicopters to air-deliver radars and equipment. The wing's 21st Tactical Air Support Squadron (TASS) 'Raven FACs' operated O-2As and OV-10As (black fin cap on OV-10s, nil on O-2As) at the start of the decade, but transferred its OV-10As to other units during 1980. Its remaining O-2As adopted 'SR' codes from 1984 and converted to the OT-37B 'Tweet FAC' during 1986. The OT-37B, intended as a stopgap O-2A replacement was unique to 21st TASS. Twenty-nine were converted from T-37B trainers, equipped with VHF-FM radios and painted in tactical 'European One' camouflage. From 1988 21st TASS reverted to the OV-10A; the OT-37Bs were converted back to standard T-37B trainer configuration. Their OV-10As initially had a blue/yellow checkerboard tail stripe, later a blue stripe with 'RAVEN' titles. The unit converted to the OA-10A during 1991. The 703d Tactical Air Support Squadron (Helicopter) (TASS(H)) 'The Magnificent Men' flew CH-3E helicopters ('VA', replaced by 'SR' in 1985). The squadron inactivated 1 June 1988. The wing provided TACPs to support the 82d Airborne Division during Operation Urgent Fury over Grenada in 1983.

The 549th Tactical Air Support Training Group (TASTG) at Patrick AFB, Florida, ('FL'/red from 1984; 'PF'/yellow from 1987), controlled 549th Tactical Air Support Training Squadron (TASTS). This was the FAC RTU with O-2As (until 1986) and OV-10As. It inactivated 1 July 1988, briefly adding a few OT-37Bs loaned from the 21st TASS for a few months beforehand. OV-10A training transferred to the 22d TASTS (q.v.).

The final 9th AF flying wing during the 1980s was the 1st Special Operations Wing (SOW) at Eglin Air Force Auxiliary Field No. 9 (Hurlburt Field), Florida. It was assigned the 8th Special Operations Squadrons (SOS) with MC-130E 'Combat Talon I', the 16th SOS with AC-130H Spectre gunships and the 20th SOS with CH-3E and UH-1N helicopters. The CH-3Es were replaced by the HH-53H from 17 June 1980, the last CH-3E leaving during September 1980. A trio of 8th SOS MC-130Es participated in Operation Eagle Claw on 24/25 April 1980, the attempted rescue of US hostages in Iran. They carried a 118-man Delta Force assault group to the 'Desert One'

A Tactical Air Control Party (TACP) training during 1989. Sgt Gary E. Parks, tactical air command and control specialist, left, determines coordinates for an air strike while ground forward air controller 1st Lt Eric Wickson radios his airborne counterpart. Both are members of the 21st TASS, 507th TAIRCW. (NARA)

A 21st TASS, 507th TAIRCW OV-10A Bronco fires 2.75-inch white phosphorus unguided rockets to mark a target for an air strike during the same 1989 tactical air control training exercise seen in the previous image. (NARA)

An 8th SOS, 1st SOW, MC-130E-C 'Combat Talon I' at low-level over the Arizona desert during 1980. Note the special green and black camouflage scheme used by MC-130Es at this time. (NARA)

A 16th SOS, 1st SOW, AC-130H at Kwangju Air Base in the Republic of Korea during Exercise Team Spirit '81. Armament consists of a pair of M61 20mm cannon forward plus a 40mm Bofors cannon and 105mm Howitzer to the rear. Sensors include the AN/ASD-5 'Black Crow' ignition sensor in the radome on the left forward fuselage, the AN/ASQ-24A 'Stabilized Tracking Set' in the left forward doorway and the AN/APQ-150 Beacon tracking radar in the rear left side radome. The air data probe protruding from the right side of the nose was later deleted from AC-130Hs. It is in overall FS 36118 'Gunship Gray'. (NARA)

A 20th SOS, 1st SOW CH-3E at Hurlburt Field during Exercise J-Catch, a 1979 joint rotary and fixed-wing tactics development and capability evaluation. Camouflage is the 'Leopard' scheme of FS 34102 light green, FS 34092 dark green and FS 30118 brown spots over an FS 36231 grey base. (NARA)

Three 20th SOS, 1st SOW UH-1Ns during J-Catch in 1979. The lead 'Huey' wears non-standard camouflage of dark green/medium grey uppers and light grey undersides, the second has the 'Leopard' camouflage scheme while the third is in an early form of 'European I' camouflage. (NARA)

forward staging area, from where they would be taken to their final objective in USN RH-53D helicopters. Unserviceability of several RH-53Ds resulted in the decision to abort at 'Desert One' where tragedy and debacle then struck; a RH-53D collided with a 7th ACCS EC-130E (ABCCC) acting as a ground tanker, resulting in the death of eight Americans and the abandonment of the remaining RH-53Ds. Survivors withdrew in the MC-130Es and remaining EC-130Es. Four 16th SOS AC-130Hs had deployed to Wadi Qena airfield in Egypt for Eagle Claw, in case they were required to move forward to provide support. USAF Special Operations units were reorganised following Eagle Claw; MAC activated Twenty-Third Air Force (23d AF) on 1 March 1983 to control these units. Consequently 1st SOW transferred from TAC to 2d AD, 23d AF, MAC on that date.

On 1 January 1983 United States Central Command Air Forces (CENTAF) was established. This was a co-designation used for 9th AF assets assigned to United States Central Command (which had activated the same date, replacing RDJTF).

# Twelfth Air Force

Twelfth Air Force (12th AF, headquarters Bergstrom AFB, Texas) held TAC's assets in the western contiguous USA, plus those in Panama. As a number of bases were home to more than one wing, during December 1980–January 1981, four Air Divisions were activated to act as an intermediate command level between those wings and 12th AF headquarters.

The following 12th AF wings reported directly to 12th AF HQ.

The F-111D-equipped 27th TFW ('CC') at Cannon AFB, New Mexico controlled the 481st TFTS 'Green Knights' (green), the 522d TFS 'Fireballs' (red), 523d TFS 'Crusaders' (blue) and the 524th TFS 'Hounds of Heaven' (yellow). The 481st TFTS was the F-111D RTU until 8 July 1980 when it inactivated and the 524th became the RTU (as 524th TFTS). On 2 April 1990 the 428th TFTS, was activated under 27th TFW, operating F-111Gs (modified ex-SAC FB-1111As). This was the only USAF unit to use the F-111G during its brief three-year USAF career.

The F-111D was originally intended to be the definitive variant. The initial F-111A had introduced TFR, fully integrated into the automatic flight control system, allowing for 'hands-off' high speed flight down to 200 feet; still a rare capability even by the 1980s. However, its Mk1 analogue avionics were relatively simple, not much

A 522d TFS, 27th TFW F-111D at George AFB during Red Flag '80-1. The F-111 fleet retained SEA camouflage to the end of the 1980s, the F-111 version of SEA replacing the light grey undersides with FS 37038 black. All TAC aircraft replaced white markings (tail code, serial number etc), as seen here, with black markings in the early 1980s to reduce visibility. From 1990 the F-111 fleet slowly adopted overall FS 36118 grey. (NARA)

A 523d TFS, 27th TFW F-111D over the Republic of Korea during Exercise Team Spirit '85. By this time black markings had long since replaced white ones. (NARA)

more sophisticated than F-4C avionics. The USAF wanted something more advanced. The F-111D was the result, with Rockwell Mk2 digital avionics, but it was too much of a technological leap. Massively delayed, and problematic for several years after finally entering service, the F-111D became known as the 'Dog'. These delays resulted in development of the F-111E using older Mk1 analogue avionics; the F-111E entered service before the F-111D. A final strike model, F-111F, utilised hybrid digital/analogue avionics. The F-111E/Fs eventually ended up serving with USAFE, leaving TAC with the F-111A/Ds. Typical F-111 weapons were Mk 82/84 slick or retarded bombs, cluster bombs, BLU-107 Durandal anti-runway bombs and B57 or B61 tactical nuclear bombs. An ECM pod could be carried under the rear fuselage. TAC F-111A/D models lacked precision guided munition capability as later gained by USAFE F-111Fs.

The 67th TRW ('BA') at Bergstrom AFB, Texas, conducted tactical reconnaissance with the RF-4C, assigned the 12th TRS 'Blackbirds' (orange) and the 91st TRS (red). These squadrons inactivated on 30 September 1992 and 30 August 1991 respectively. During 1982 the RF-4C RTU function and Phantom reconnaissance school moved from 363d TRW to 67th TRW; the 45th TRTS 'Polka Dots' (blue) activated on 1 April 1982 (Inactivating on 30 September 1989), while the 62d TRTS (yellow) transferred from the 363d TRW to the 67th TRW on 1 July 1982 (inactivating on 31 December 1989).

The 366th TFW ('MO') at Mountain Home AFB, Idaho, operated F-111As. Assigned squadrons were the 389th TFTS 'Thunderbolts' (yellow) the F-111A RTU (inactivated 22 July 1991), 390th TFS 'Boars' (green; inactivated 1 October 1982) and the 391st TFS 'Bold Tigers' (blue; inactivated 1 July 1990). The wing had been assigned the 388th TFTS as the F-111A RTU until 30 September 1979 when it was inactivated, on which date the 389th TFS took over the mission and became a TFTS as above. The 388th was reactivated on 1 July 1981 as TAC's first EF-111A Raven unit, as the 388th Electronic Combat Squadron (ECS) 'Griffins'. It inactivated again on 15 December 1982, replaced by 390th ECS 'Ravens', which took on the 388th's personnel and equipment. The electronic warfare EF-111A, modified from surplus F-111As, integrated the AN/ALQ-99E radar jamming system, a repackaged version of the USN's EA-6B Prowler's system. The 390th ECS deployed EF-111As to jam enemy radars during Operation Just Cause in Panama.

A 524th TFS, 27th TFW F-111D departs MacDill AFB in 1987 after the conclusion of the Long Rifle III competition. The F-111's bulky main undercarriage is apparent. (NARA)

A 522d TFS, 27th TFW F-111D four-ship over the Giza pyramids during Bright Star '83 in Egypt. (NARA)

A 12th TRS, 67th TRW, RF-4C arriving at Zweibrucken AB, West Germany for Salty Bee '84. The unit deployed eighteen RF-4Cs for the exercise, between 16 May and 14 June 1984. The aircraft is in 'European I' camouflage. The visor housing of the crew's HGU-26/P helmets are in orange, the squadron colour. (NARA)

A 45th TRTS, 67th TRW, RF-4C over western Texas while competing in Reconnaissance Air Meet '86. (NARA)

Another 45th TRTS, 67th TRW, RF-4C, over Texas during 1988. By now 'Hill Gray II' camouflage had replaced 'European I'. The two-tone, medium (FS 26270) and dark (FS 26118) grey, 'Hill Gray II' scheme was very similar, but not identical, to the three-tone light, medium and dark grey factory-applied F-16 scheme. Subsequently F-16s would adopt the simplified two tone 'Hill Gray II' scheme by dropping the light grey undersides in favour of medium grey. (NARA)

A 391st TFS, 366th TFW, F-111A leads a pair of Republic of Korea Air Force F-4Ds while deployed to South Korea during 1978. The F-111A carries live Mk 82 LDGP bombs under its inner pylon and a SUU-20 practice bomb dispenser under the outer pylon. (NARA)

A 391st TFS, 366th TFW, F-111A seen in 1980 with a full load of twenty-four live Mk82 LDGP 500lb bombs, heading to Nellis Air Force Range. The aircraft retains white tail markings, which would soon be replaced by black ones. (NARA)

Two 390th ECS, 366th TFW, EF-111As taxi at Sachon AB in the Republic of Korea, while deployed for Team Spirit '85. (NARA)

A 390th ECS, 366th TFW, EF-111A en route to Eglin AFB for Solid Shield '87. EF-111As wore a standard scheme of FS 36492 'Pearl Gray' sides and undersides and FS 36320 'Compass Ghost Gray' upper sides. (NARA)

The 388th TFW ('HL') at Hill AFB, Utah, was completing re-equipment from F-4Ds to F-16A/Bs at the turn of the decade. Its F-4D-equipped 4th TFS 'Fightin' Fuujins' (yellow) converted to early Block F-16A/Bs April–June 1980, F-16A/B Block 15s during spring 1983 and F-16C/D Block 40s during 1989/90. The 16th TFTS (blue, switching to blue/white checkerboard in 1982) with early F-16A/Bs became the 16th TFS on 1 April 1983 and received F-16A/B Block 15s. It inactivated on 30 June 1986. The 34th TFS (red) with F-16A/Bs briefly served as an RTU without 'TFTS' designation. It upgraded to F-16A/B Block 15s in late 1983/early 1984 and received F-16C/D Block 40s during 1989. Finally, the 421st TFS (black) had recently retired F-4Ds and was non-operational from spring 1979 until receiving early F-16A/Bs in August 1980. It received F-16A/B Block 15s in December 1982/January 1983 and F-16C/D Block 40s from 1990.

A very early F-16A Block 1, easily identifiable due to its black radome, of the 16th TFTS, 388th TFW, deployed to Holloman AFB for Exercise Border Star '81. This aircraft, 78-0017, was the seventeenth production F-16A. (NARA)

An F-16A Block 5 of the 34th TFS, 388th TFW carries a single CATM-9J during Border Star '81. During this exercise a new pilot flying another 388th TFW F-16A ran out of fuel and decided to attempt a landing on a dirt road. He changed his mind at the last moment and ejected. However, the now unmanned F-16A landed almost intact (breaking off the TACAN antenna under the intake) and was later recovered and repaired. The young Lieutenant pilot was not so lucky, apparently losing his wings. (NARA)

A newly received F-16A Block 5 of the 4th TFS, 388th TFW seen during 1980 carrying captive training Sidewinders (wingtip CATM-9Ls, inboard CATM-9Js) and live 2000lb Mk 84 LDGP bombs, plus 370 US gal underwing fuel tanks and a centreline ALQ-119 ECM pod. The aircraft was on its way to the Nellis Air Force Range to drop the Mk 84s. (NARA)

A joint USAF and EAF formation passes over the pyramids during Bright Star '82. A 353d TFS, 354th TFW A-10A leads an EAF UTI-MiG-15, a 388th TFW F-16A Block 10 (in wing commander's markings) and finally an EAF MiG-21PFM. (NARA)

The 4th TFS, 388th TFW replaced its early F-16As with F-16A Block 15s in early 1983. Here eight 4th TFS F-16A Block 15s are seen deployed to Flesland Air Station, Norway for Exercise Coronet Colt. The unit deployed twelve F-16As for Coronet Colt between 27 August and 24 September 1984. (NARA)

The 474th TFW ('NA') at Nellis AFB, Nevada re-equipped from F-4Ds to F-16A/Bs during 1980/1. The 428th TFS 'Buccaneers' (blue) converted from F-4Ds to F-16A/B Block 10s during October 1980. It inactivated 30 June 1989. The 429th TFS 'Black Falcons' (yellow, replaced by black from 1985) received its first F-16A/B Block 10s from 20 February 1981. It inactivated on 30 September 1989. Finally, the 430th TFS 'Tigers'/'The Beachball Squadron' (red) received F-16A/B Block 10s from 27 May 1981. It inactivated 1 July 1989. Defence cuts, plus overcrowding at Nellis, resulted in the wing inactivating on 30th September 1989.

The following Air Divisions were activated during 1980/1 to control 12th AF wings at 'dual wing' bases.

At George AFB, California, 831st Air Division (AD) activated on 1 December 1980, replacing 'Tactical Training, George'. It controlled the 35th TFW ('GA'/'WW') conducting fighter, RTU and 'Wild Weasel' Suppression of Enemy Air Defences (SEAD) operations. It became 35th TTW on 1 July 1984, reverting to 35th TFW on 5 October 1989. 831st AD also controlled the 37th TFW from 30 March 1981 to 5 October 1989, which took over the 35th TFW's 'Wild Weasel' elements between those dates.

The 35th TFW controlled the following squadrons. The 20th TFTS (blue; after 1981 silver/'GA') operated German-owned F-4Es, providing Luftwaffe F-4F crew training. The unit's Luftwaffe element was known as 1. Deutsche Luftwaffenausbildungsstaffel USA (1. DtLwAusbStff USA - 1st German Air Force Training Squadron USA). The 21st TFTS (black, 'GA') with F-4Es became the combat-coded 21st TFS on 9 October 1980 before reverting to 21st TFTS (as an RTU) on 1 July 1983. The 39th TFTS (white/'WW') operated F-4Gs. It transferred its assets to the 562d TFTS (q.v.) on 9 October 1980, and was redesignated the 39th TFS the same day, but non-operational until 6 January 1982 when it converted to Pave Spike laser designator pod equipped

A 429th TFS, 474th TFW F-16A Block 10 'hot pit' refuelling (i.e. without shutting its engine down, allowing for a quicker turn-around) at RAF Bentwaters during Exercise Coronet Wrangler in 1982. It carries CATM-9Ls, SUU-20s and 370 US gal fuel tanks. The 429th TFS deployed eleven F-16As and a single F-16B for Coronet Wrangler between 13 April and 7 May 1982. This was a troubled deployment. In mid-April USAF F-16s which had completed more than 200 hours were grounded, causing cancellation of the 429th's planned involvement in RAF air defence exercise 'Elder Forest'. Then on 4 May one of their F-16As crashed near Beccles, Norfolk. Fortunately the pilot ejected. (NARA)

429th TFS, 474th TFW F-16A Block 10s deployed to Homestead AFB during Solid Shield '87. The underwing Triple Ejector Racks (TERs) have been loaded with BDU-33 25-pound practice 'blue bombs'. (NARA)

The 474th TFW wing commander's F-16A Block 10 during Solid Shield '87. It carries CATM-9Ls, inert Mk 82 practice bombs (formally known as BDU-50s) in a 'flat 2' arrangement on the TERs and 370 US gal underwing tanks. (NARA)

474th TFW F-16A Block 10s over the Grand Canyon during 1986. The wing commander's aircraft leads aircraft marked for the squadron commanders of the 428th, 429th and 430th TFS. The latter three aircraft have dual TFS/AMU markings, AMU being the aligned Aircraft Maintenance Unit. (NARA)

F-4Es (ex-21st TFW aircraft from Alaska) with 'GA'/gold tail stripe as a combat-coded unit. It inactivated on 11 May 1984. The 561st TFS (yellow) served briefly as an F-4E RTU, then combat-coded with F-4Gs ('WW') from 1 October 1980. It was reassigned to the 37th TFW 30 March 1981 (with mixed F-4E/G fleet) and reassigned back to the 35th TFW on 5 October 1989 (with a pure F-4G fleet). It retained yellow throughout and 'WW' from 1 October 1980 onwards. The 562d TFS (green) operated F-105Gs with 'GA' tail codes, changing to 'WW' in the final months of F-105G operations. Redesignated 562d TFTS on 9 October 1980 with a mixed F-4E/G fleet (white/'WW') it was reassigned to the 37th TFW on 30 March 1981 retaining F-4E/Gs (blue/'WW'). It was reassigned back to 35th TFW 5 October 1989 (retaining blue/'WW'). The 563d TFS (red/'WW') operated F-4Gs, was reassigned to the 37th TFW 30 March 1981 but did not return to the 35th TFW with the other squadrons. The 35th TFW/TTW also had a pair of UH-1Ps (in the South East Asia camouflage scheme with 'GA') directly assigned to the wing for support duties. There were replaced in 1980 by a pair of ex-Minot AFB/Det 7, 37th ARRS (MAC) UH-1Fs, retaining their blue rescue colour scheme at George. The 'Hueys' primarily flew support crews from George to nearby Cuddeback Air-to-Ground Gunnery Range, plus other support and medivac duties. Helicopter support operations terminated 1987.

The 37th TFW ('WW') activated on 30 March 1981. As outlined above three 35th TFW 'Wild Weasel' squadrons were reassigned to the 37th on that date; 561st TFS (yellow), 562d TFTS (blue) and 563d TFS (red), all three with mixed F-4E/G fleets. On 5 October 1989 the 561st TFS and 562d TFTS returned to the 35th TFW, while the 563d TFS inactivated.

Following an initial prototype conversion F-4G 'Wild Weasel V', this aircraft (69-7263) became the first 'production' conversion. It is seen in 1978 serving with the F-4G project test force (ongoing F-4G testing would soon be taken over by Det 5, TAWC). Consequently, while in 35th TFW markings, it is not assigned to a 35th TFW squadron and displays no squadron colours or markings. It is seen carrying an ATM-45 (a captive training AGM-45 Shrike) and an ALQ-119 ECM pod. (NARA)

A 563d TFS, 35th TFW F-4G at George AFB during 1979. The F-4G introduced the F-15's 'high g' 600 US gal tank in lieu of the usual centreline F-4 600 US gal tank, a feature later extended to all USAF Phantoms apart from F-4C models. This allowed heavily laden F-4Gs to violently pop up to acquire their targets and dip back down to low-level again. The extensive stencilling on various panels is notable. (NARA)

Another 563d TFS, 35th TFW, F-4G during 1980. By now white markings had given way to black. Trials had found that replacing white stencils, serial numbers and tail codes with black ones considerably reduced an aircraft's visual signature. An ATM-45 training round is under the wing. (NARA)

A normally marked 20th TFTS F-4E leads F-4Es in 20th TFTS/AMU and 35th TTW flagship markings during 1987. The 20th TFTS operated West German owned F-4E airframes to train Luftwaffe F-4F crews. (NARA)

The 'European I' camouflaged belly of the 35th TTW wing commander's flagship F-4E. It carries a pair of CATM-9Ps and a centreline tank. (NARA)

A pair of 21st TFTS, 35th TTW, F-4Es in formation with a 2nd Bombardment Wing B-52G (the second Phantom just visible behind the B-52's rear fuselage). The CATM-9P toting F-4Es were conducting an air defence training mission during the first 'Shootout' conventional bombing competition, held by SAC's 15th Air Force in 1989. The B-52G is in SAC's B-52 Strategic Camouflage Scheme, the SAC equivalent of 'European I' worn by tactical aircraft and seen on these F-4Es. The SAC scheme consisted of upper sides in FS 34086 green and FS 36081 grey and undersides in FS 36081 grey and FS 36118 grey. (NARA)

A 563d TFS, 35th TFW, F-4G seen in January 1981. Two months later, this squadron, along with the 561st TFS and 562d TFTS would be reassigned to the 37th TFW. It carries an AGM-78D Standard ARM, an ALQ-119 ECM pod and a centreline tank. (NARA)

The same F-4G in the previous image, now seen in 1982. The 563d TFS was by then reassigned to the 37th TFW. Note the 37th TFW emblem on the intake side, replacing the 35th TFW one. A toned-down version of the squadron's emblem (a sabre passing through an ace of spades playing card on a red background) is painted on the front of the tail. It appears that the aircraft has been at least partially repainted since the earlier image (note the larger area of dark green on the forward fuselage). It carries an ATM-45 training round, an ALQ-119 ECM pod and the usual centreline F-15 'high g' 600 US gal tank. (NARA)

A pair of 561st TFS, 37th TFW F-4Gs wait their turn to refuel from a SAC KC-135A while a pair of 339th TFS, 347th TFW, F-4Es are refuelled during Gallant Eagle '82. The F-4Gs carry ATM-78Ds (captive training versions of the AGM-78D Standard). (NARA)

Converted from F-4E airframes, the F-4G 'Wild Weasel V' became the last frontline USAF Phantom II variant introduced. At its heart was the AN/APR-38 RHAW (Radar Homing And Warning) system, part of which displaced the former F-4E's gun. AN/APR-38 was squadron-reprogrammable, being updateable to recognise all known air defence radar systems, displaying their locations in predetermined priority order to the crew. Targets could then be engaged by anti-radiation missiles (ARMs); initially AGM-45A/B Shrike or AGM-78D Standard, the latter replaced by AGM-88A HARM (High-speed Anti-Radiation Missile) by 1984. The less effective Shrikes remained in the inventory into the 1990s. Different Shrike sub-variants were required to target different radar systems and its limited range required it to be fired well within the range of enemy SAM sites. HARM addressed these deficiencies, while adding much increased speed, allowing targets to be struck before they could react. Improved AGM-88B HARMs were added by the end of the decade. F-4Gs could also use the usual air-to-ground ordnance, including bombs/CBUs, AGM-65 and GBU-15. From 1987 F-4Gs were upgraded to 'Wild Weasel VI' configuration, receiving much improved AN/APR-47 RHAW. With a threefold increase in computer memory (to 250K), it was able to analyse threats five times faster, requiring F-4Gs to spend less time during 'pop ups' from low-level flight to acquire targets.

The previously secret F-117A 'stealth fighters' of the 4450th TG at Tonopah had recently been made public, and the 37th TFW unit identity (available since the

Four F-4Es of the 37th TFW Gunsmoke '85 team. As the competition involved gunnery as well as bombing, the F-4G was precluded from participating, consequently the wing's F-4Es were entered. As was common for wings entering teams for Gunsmoke, the team was formed from personnel and aircraft from across the wing. Aircraft were prepared to a high standard for the competition, with paintwork touched up; occasionally aircraft were completely repainted. Special markings replaced the usual individual squadron markings. In this case this was red/yellow/blue fin stripes (representing the wing's three squadrons) plus a white 'shadow' added to the tail markings, usually the preserve of a unit commander's 'flagship' aircraft. (NARA)

The 37th TFW wing commander's F-4G leads the 561st TFS commander's F-4G in 1988, a year before the F-4Gs transferred back to the 35th TFW. By now the wing had started to adopt 'Hill Gray II' camouflage. The lead F-4G carries four live AGM-88 HARM missiles, his wingman carries four older, live, AGM-45 Shrike ARMs. Both carry ALQ-184 ECM pods in the forward left Sparrow well, two Sparrows in the rear wells and a centreline tank. (NARA)

The HARM-toting 37th TFW wing commander's F-4G seen in the previous image. It is fitted with the very rare one-piece windscreen, which replaced the original three-piece windscreen normally found on Phantoms. This greatly improved both windscreen bird-strike resistance and pilot visibility. Originally considered for adoption across the USAF F-4 fleet, ultimately only twenty-one USAF F-4s were so modified before the upgrade was cancelled; seven each F-4Es, F-4Gs and RF-4Cs. (NARA)

'Wild Weasel' mission reverted to 35th TFW) was used to replace the provisional 4450th TG identity on 5 October 1989. The 37th TFW henceforth reported directly to 12th AF. On the same date three new squadrons activated; the 415th TFS 'Nightstalkers' with F-117As (the former 4450th TS), the 416th TFS 'Ghostriders' with F-117As (the former 4451st TS) and the 417th TFTS 'Bandits' with F-117As and T-38As (the former 4453d TS, RTU).

The 832d AD activated on 1 December 1980 at Luke AFB, Arizona, replacing 'Tactical Training, Luke' which had hitherto controlled the resident training units. Subordinate components at Luke were the 58th TTW and 405th TTW.

The 58th TTW controlled F-4 ('LA') and later F-16 ('LF', for 'Luke Falcon') RTUs, plus a German Starfighter training unit. The 69th TFTS (no squadron colour/code) trained German personnel on the F-104G/TF-104G, having an alternate Luftwaffe designation of 2. Deutsche Luftwaffenausbildungsstaffel USA (2. DtLwAusbStff USA – 2nd German Air Force Training Squadron USA). With German Starfighter operations concluding, the unit inactivated on 16 March 1983. It held forty-five in-service airframes, plus twenty-one in storage, at the time of inactivation. The 310th TFTS (green/'LA') operated the F-4C until 29 June 1982. After a pause it converted to F-16A/Bs in January 1983 ('LF') re-equipping with F-16C/Ds during 1991. The 311th TFTS 'Sidewinders' (blue/'LA') also ceased F-4C operations on 29 June 1982 and converted to F-16A/Bs during 1983 ('LF'). It supported Republic of Singapore Air Force F-16 training under 'PEACE CARVIN' from 4 March 1988 until 3 January 1990. In 1991 it replaced its F-16A/Bs with former 312th TFTS (q.v.) F-16C/D Block 42s, upon the latter's inactivation. The 426th TFTS (yellow/'LA') ceased F-4C operations in late 1980 and transferred to the 405th TTW on 1 January 1981 with F-15s. On 1 October 1984 the 312th TFTS (black/red, 'LF') activated with F-16C/D Block 25s, upgrading to Block 42s in 1990. On 1 October 1986 the 314th TFTS (yellow/black, 'LF') activated with F-16C/D Block 25s, retaining these until inactivating in 1994. Until they were reassigned to 405th TTW on 29 August 1979 the 58th TTW had also controlled the 550th and 555th TFTSs.

The 405th TTW ('LA' code) controlled F-15 RTUs (equipped with F-15A/B/Ds, but no F-15Cs; becoming F-15E RTUs from 1988) plus an F-5 unit. The latter was

Some 58th TTW variety on 1 August 1979. A 550th TFTS F-15A leads a 310th TFTS F-4C, a 69th TFTS F-104G Starfighter and a 425th TFTS F-5E. The 69th TFTS trained West German Starfighter aircrew, while the 425th TFTS trained allied F-5 aircrew. All were based at Luke AFB, apart from the 425th that was detached at Williams AFB. This was immediately prior to reorganisation which saw the 405th TTW activated on 29 August 1979, the new wing absorbing the 58th TTW's F-15 and F-5 squadrons. (NARA)

Three 69th TFTS, 58th TTW, F-104Gs return to Luke AFB after a visit to the bombing range in November 1982, each carrying a centreline SUU-21 practice bomb dispenser. SUU-21 was originally developed for use by USAFE, with added safety precautions due to the requirement to regularly fly over populated areas in Europe. It carried the practice bombs within an enclosed bay (unlike the earlier SUU-20 in which the practice bombs were carried exposed) and they were spring ejected (rather than explosively ejected as in the SUU-20). The 69th TFTS trained West German Luftwaffe (Air Force) and Marine (Navy) aircrew in West German owned, US marked, aircraft and disbanded in March 1983. (NARA)

58th TTW F-16A Block 10s and F-16C Block 25s in 1987, each in unit commander's markings. From the nearest they are a 314th TFTS F-16C, a 312th TFTS F-16C, a 311th TFTS F-16A, a 310th TFTS F-16A and the 58th TTW wing commander's F-16A. They carry no underwing pylons or stores, only wingtip CATM-9Ls. (NARA)

A 58th TTW and 405th TTW formation over the Grand Canyon in 1987. A 405th TTW F-15A marked as the 832d Air Division flagship leads another F-15A in 405th TTW flagship markings and a 425th TFTS F-5E, while nearest the camera is the 58th TTW flagship F-16A Block 10. (NARA)

the 425th TFTS 'Freedom Fighters' that was detached at Williams AFB, Arizona, operating F-5B/E/F models. It trained allied nations' F-5 pilots and acted as an RTU for USAF F-5 pilots either destined for the Aggressors or an advisor posting to allied F-5 operating nations. It inactivated on 1 September 1989. The 461st TFTS 'Deadly Jesters' (yellow) operated F-15A/Bs, converting to F-15Es on 12 April 1988. The 550th TFTS 'Phoenix Phantoms' (black/silver) operated F-15A/Bs, converting to F-15Es during March 1989. The 555th TFTS (green) had F-15A/Bs, converting to F-15Es during 1991. As mentioned above, on 1 January 1981 the 426th TFTS 'Killer Claws' (previously operating F-4Cs with the 58th TTW) transferred to the 405th TTW (adopting a red tail stripe) and operating F-15A/B/Ds. It inactivated on 29 November 1990. Finally, a small number of 'LA' coded UH-1F/Ps were directly assigned to the wing until such operations terminated in 1987.

The 833d AD at Holloman AFB, New Mexico activated on 1 December 1980, replacing 'Tactical Training, Holloman', controlling a combat-coded F-15 wing and a 'Lead In Fighter Training' (LIFT) wing.

The resident 49th TFW ('HO') controlled the 7th TFS 'Bunyaps' (blue), 8th TFS 'Black Sheep' (yellow) and the 9th TFS 'Iron Knights' (red). These operated the F-15A/B (never upgrading to later C/D models).

The 479th TTW ('HM') conducted AT-38B LIFT operations with the 416th TFTS (silver), 434th TFTS (red), 435th TFTS (blue) and 436th TFTS (yellow). On 1 September 1983 the 416th TFTS was inactivated and replaced by the 433d TFTS (green); the latter had previously been the 433d FWS under 57th TTW at Nellis AFB (q.v.). LIFT allowed new pilots to learn fighter basics in a familiar aircraft (after completing advanced training in Air Training Command's T-38A trainers). AT-38Bs were modified from T-38As by adding a gunsight and centreline practice bomb dispenser.

Lieutenant Colonel Hollis K. Fox, commander of the 550th TFTS, takes his squadron flagship F-15A low over a mesa near Monument Valley in 1987. (NARA)

A 425th TFTS, 405th TTW, F-5E flown by Major John S. Woodward in 1987. The unit had by then moved away from its former high-visibility (aluminium with yellow bands) to overall grey with toned-down markings. In the early 1980s a number of camouflaged F-5s were used by the unit, including SEA camouflaged aircraft. (NARA)

A formation of 405th TTW F-15As near Phoenix, Arizona in 1987. From the nearest they are the flagships of the 461st TFTS, 426th TFTS, 405th TTW, 550th TFTS and 555th TFTS. Between 1988 and 1991 three of these squadrons became F-15E RTUs, while the 426th inactivated. (NARA)

A 49th TFW F-4D arrives at Ramstein AB, West Germany for Crested Cap '77. The 49th was reassigned from USAFE/Spangdahlem to TAC/Holloman in 1968. It was designated as 'dual-based', ready to immediately return to Germany in an emergency, practiced annually during 'Crested Cap'. For Crested Cap '77 8th TFS deployed twenty-four F-4Ds (22 August to 22 September) and 9th TFS deployed twenty-six F-4Ds (11 September to 10 October), attached to 86th TFW/USAFE at Ramstein. Squadrons commonly borrowed aircraft from other squadrons in the wing for such deployments, hence this 7th TFS (blue fin stripe) F-4D in the initial 8th TFS deployment. This was the 49th TFW's last Crested Cap; from October 1977, immediately after Crested Cap '77, the wing started transitioning to air superiority F-15s. Thereafter the F-4E equipped 4th TFW took over the commitment, until 1982 when Crested Cap was opened up to other TAC units. (NARA)

A 8th TFS, 49th TFW F-15A shows off its load of live AIM-9L Sidewinders and AIM-7F Sparrows in 1980. (NARA)

A pair of 7th TFS, 49th TFW, F-15As during 1988. The nearest aircraft is the squadron flagship. (NARA)

A 434th TFTS, 479th TTW AT-38B carrying an SUU-20 practice bomb dispenser. The three-tone camouflage adopted by the AT-38Bs was nicknamed 'Smurf Jet' by crews and consisted of FS 15164 'Gray', FS 15450 'Light Blue' and FS 15109 'Dark Blue'. (NARA)

The 836th AD at Davis-Monthan AFB, Arizona activated on 1 January 1981, replacing 'Tactical Training, Davis-Monthan', which had hitherto controlled the resident 355th TTW ('DM'), assigned A-10A RTUs: 333d TFTS (red), 357th TFTS (yellow) and 358th TFTS (green). The wing was previously the A-7D RTU, replacing the last of these during 1979.

'Tactical Training, Davis-Monthan' had also controlled the 432d Tactical Drone Group at Davis-Monthan until it inactivated on 1 April 1979. The wing's 11th and 22d Tactical Drone Squadrons had used photographic reconnaissance AQM-34L/M/V tactical drones, supported by DC-130 launch aircraft and CH-3 recovery helicopters (only the CH-3s used 'DM' codes).

On 1 September 1982 the 602d TAIRCW moved its wing headquarters from Bergstrom AFB, Texas to Davis-Monthan and fell under 836th AD (previously reporting directly to 12th AF). The 602d TAIRCW (like 9th AF's equivalent 507th TAIRCW), was primarily concerned with managing the 'Tactical Air Control System' but included the following flying units. The 23d TASS 'Best in the West' (later 'Nail FACs') operated O-2As (with red or yellow fin tops and bottoms) and OV-10A (no colour/code) from Bergstrom. It moved to Davis-Monthan on 1 July 1980 taking over the personnel and equipment (i.e. only O-2As) of the former 27th TASS and retained their former blue or red fin top/bottoms. 23d TASS received OA-37Bs from 2 May 1981 (blue, red or yellow fin colours/'NF'). In 1987 it became the first USAF unit to re-equip with the OA-10A (blue/'NF'). It inactivated in 1991. The 27th TASS 'First In–Last Out' operated O-2As (blue or red fin top/bottom) at Davis-Monthan. It inactivated on 1 July 1980, passing its O-2As and personnel to the 23d TASS. It reactivated on 15 May 1984 with ex-USAFE (20th/704th TASS) OV-10As, detached at George AFB,

Two recently received 355th TTW A-10As on deployment to South Korea during 1977. The nearest carries two Maverick training rounds plus eight live Mark 20 Rockeye II CBUs. The other carries a live Mk 82 LDGP 'slick' bombs. They display the 'Symmetrical MASK 10A' camouflage scheme, one of several early grey A-10 schemes and the first widely adopted. It consisted of '30% MASK-10A' (dark grey) uppers and '50% MASK-10A' (light grey) undersides plus an underside false canopy in FS 36118. The grey schemes made A-10s conspicuous to enemy fighters, especially over typical European terrain. After trials 'European I' replaced the grey schemes. A decade later, the reduced air-to-air threat post-Cold War saw A-10s return to grey camouflage. (NARA)

A pair of 358th TFTS, 355th TTW, A-10As in the standard 'European I' scheme, deployed to MacDill AFB in 1987 to participate in the Long Rifle III competition. (NARA)

A 23d TASS, 602d TAIRCW, OA-37B during 1983 in wraparound SEA camouflage. It carries six external fuel tanks and a pair of LAU-68 seven-tube rocket pods. For FAC purposes these would carry 2.75 inch white phosphorus rockets for marking targets. (NARA)

The 23d TASS, 602d TAIRCW, flagship OA-10A, carrying a pair of LAU-68s in November 1987. The 23d became the first USAF OA-10A unit that year. (NARA)

A 27th TASS, 602d TAIRCW, OV-10A during 1987, carrying LAU-68 rocket pods. Its 'European I' camouflage stands out conspicuously against the Californian High Desert terrain near George AFB. (NARA)

Captain Eric Stoll pilots a 27th TASS, 602d TAIRCW, OV-10A over the Californian desert during 1987. The OV-10's excellent visibility is evident. (NARA)

California ('VV', initially with either yellow or blue tail stripes, later with yellow and blue checkerboards). The 22d TASTS (yellow/'NF'), activated 14 October 1988, was the TASS RTU, operating a mixture of OV-10As and OA-10As. It inactivated in 1991. The 701st TASS(H) operated CH-53Cs (no colour/code) from Bergstrom until it inactivated 31 January 1980.

The introduction of the BGM-109G GLCM (Ground Launched Cruise Missile) into USAFE service in the 1980s required the formation of a US-based training unit under TAC. The 868th Tactical Missile Training Squadron (TMTS) activated on 1 July 1981 at Davis-Monthan AFB, Arizona under direct 12th AF control. On 1 November 1985 the 868th Tactical Missile Training Group (TMTG) activated at Davis-Monthan to control the 868th TMTS and was assigned to 836th AD.

Until 1976 United States Air Forces Southern Command had been responsible for Panama Canal Zone defence, plus wider USAF Foreign Military Sales programme and humanitarian relief operations throughout Latin America. On 1 January 1976, due to the post-Vietnam War USAF drawdown, Southern Command inactivated as a MAJCOM and TAC took over much of the mission. USAF Southern Air Division at Howard AFB, Panama activated directly under TAC HQ on 1 January 1976, absorbing these duties. On 31 January 1987 USAF Southern Air Division was reassigned to 12th AF control; it was redesignated 830th Air Division on 1 January 1989. It moved its HQ from Howard AFB to Albrook AFS, Panama on 1 March 1989. On 15 February 1991 it was redesignated Air Forces Panama and returned to Howard AFB.

The 24th Composite Wing (CW) at Howard AFB, Panama, ('HW' from 1985) was responsible for USAF operations at that base as well as Albrook AFS. The 24th CW inactivated on 31 January 1987, its components reassigned directly to USAF Southern Air Division; 24th CW reactivated on 1 January 1989, reassuming control of its former components. The 24th CW's flying unit was the 24th Composite Squadron (CS) 'Golden Jaguars' with the O-2A and UH-1N (no tail colour/code). The UH-1Ns could be operated in 'gunship' configuration with rocket pods and operated in Special Operations and general support roles. With the 1983 reassignment of Special Operations assets to MAC, the UH-1Ns were reassigned to Det 1, 2d AD, 23d AF, MAC on 1 March 1983, remaining located at Howard, until ceasing operations in 1987. The 24th CS O-2As were replaced by OA-37Bs between September 1985 and June 1986, adopting 'HW'/blue tail stripe (although 'HW' was not universally applied to their OA-37Bs). The unit was redesignated the 24th TASS on 1 January 1987 and inactivated in 1991. The 24th CW inevitably supported Operation Just Cause in Panama, including 24th TASS OA-37Bs flying FAC and CAS missions in conjunction with ANG A-7Ds.

The 24th CW also had a number of attached 'Elements' controlling rotational deployments by reserve units to Panama. These were the 'AFRES and ANG C-130 Rotational Element' (attached 1 October 1977–1 December 1984), the 'ANG A-7 Rotational Element' (attached from 1 October 1978–31 January 1987) and the 'ANG A-10 Rotational Element' (attached during 1985 and 1989). Finally, the 24th CW controlled the Inter-American Air Forces Academy (IAAFA) at Albrook AFS, which provided military education and training to military personnel of partner Latin American nations. It moved to Homestead AFB, Florida, in 1989; Hurricane Andrew's 1992 destruction there forcing its relocation to Lackland AFB, Texas.

A 24th CS, 24th CW O-2A from Howard AFB, Panama, seen during 1983 over nearby Empire Range, a US Army training facility west of the Panama Canal. LAU-68s are seen underwing. (NARA)

A 24th TASS OA-37B on deployment to Barranquilla, Columbia, in 1989 during an exchange with a *Fuerza Aérea Colombiana* (FAC: Columbian Air Force) A-37B unit. The 24th TASS regularly undertook goodwill exchanges with Latin American air forces, especially A-37B units of those air forces. (NARA)

Here a line-up of 24th TASS OA-37Bs and FAC A-37Bs is seen at Barranquilla during the 1989 deployment to Columbia. (NARA)

# Direct Reporting Units

A number of specialist units reported directly to TAC headquarters.

Tonopah Test Range Airport, Nevada was a Department of Energy airfield (utilised for nuclear weapons development) until the USAF secretly moved in during 1977, initially to operate MiGs under the secretive Project CONSTANT PEG (q.v.) for air combat training exposure of front line pilots to these enemy types. Located in the north-western corner of the Nellis Air Force Range, initial spartan facilities were improved in anticipation of the highly classified 'Senior Trend', later designated F-117A, being operated from the base.

'Senior Trend'/F-117A was a 'low observable' (LO) strike aircraft. Its primary armament consisted of LGBs, both the standard 2000lb GBU-10 Paveway II (in Mk 84 HE and BLU-109/B penetrating warhead variants), plus later a version of the improved Paveway III specially produced for the F-117A. The standard GBU-24 Paveway III 2000lb weapon features enlarged wings which would not fit in the F-117As weapons bay. Consequently GBU-27 Paveway III (featuring the BLU-109/B penetrating warhead) was produced with cropped forward canards and Paveway II's smaller rear pop-out fins. B61 tactical nuclear weapons could also be carried. The F-117A was dedicated to striking critical targets, such as key chokepoints like bridges and tunnels, enemy 'command, control, communications and intelligence' assets and nuclear storage facilities. One contingency plan, 'Downshift 02' planned to use the aircraft in Europe for enemy leadership 'decapitation' strikes, including targeting the Soviet premier's dacha.

The 4450th Tactical Group (alias the 'A-unit', an intentionally meaningless designation for everyday use) was activated on 15 October 1979 at Nellis. Four digit units were temporary MAJCOM units that were unentitled to a unit history or heritage, unlike permanent 'AFCON' (Air Force Controlled) units. On that date Det 1, 4450th TG ('Q-Unit') and Det 2, 4450th TG ('R-Unit') were also activated. Det 1 was the first unit at Tonopah. Det 2 held a number of test pilots at Burbank (later Palmdale) and Groom Lake; it later conducted acceptance checkout flights of each 'Senior Trend' plus local area familiarisation. It inactivated 30 May 1989, passing its test duties to Det 1 57th FWW and its local area familiarisation role to 4453d TES.

4450th Tactical Group pilots and maintenance crews rotated through the secret Groom Lake facility during 1981 for training, and the first squadrons (all designated as 'Test Squadrons' for cover purposes) activated at Tonopah that year. On 11 June 1981 the 4450th Test Squadron (TS) ('I-Unit') 'Nightstalkers' and 4451st TS ('P-Unit') 'Ghostriders' activated. The 4450th TS was the first operational squadron, eventually receiving the 4450th TG's first assigned F-117A on 23 August 1982. The 4451st TS did not operate F-117As, instead utilising A-7D/Ks (the only regular Air Force unit to use two-seat A-7K models) at Nellis AFB, Nevada ('LV'/black tail colour). These gave group pilots flying time prior to delivery of the F-117As, subsequently acting as chase 'companion' aircraft. During September 1982 the former Det 1, 4450th TG ('Q-Unit') was expanded into the new 4452d TS ('Q-Unit') 'Goat Suckers', the second operational squadron. Finally the 4453d Test and Evaluation Squadron (TES) ('Z-Unit') 'Grim Reapers' activated on 1 October 1985, the third 'Senior Trend' unit, acting as the RTU. In January 1989 the 4453d TES received AT-38Bs, these assumed the companion/chase role from the A-7D/Ks of the 4451st TS. As mentioned above, 4453d TES took over the local area familiarisation function from Det 2/'R-Unit' upon the latter's inactivation on 30 May 1989.

The group achieved Initial Operating Capability (IOC) on 28 October 1983 when the fourteenth F-117A was delivered. All 4450th TG F-117A flying operations were conducted during the hours of darkness as a security measure.

On 10 November 1988 the Department of Defense publicly revealed the F-117A. As mentioned above the 37th TFW at George AFB passed the 'Wild Weasel' mission back to the 35th TFW on 5 October 1989. On the same date the provisional 'MAJCOM' 4450th TG inactivated and the former group adopted the 'AFCON' 37th TFW identity (adopting 'TR'); the squadrons also adopted AFCON unit identities. The 4450th TS became the 415th TFS 'Nightstalkers' with a wartime 'Atlantic' (i.e. European) tasking. The A-7D/K-equipped 4451st TS inactivated in May 1989, its personnel forming 416th TFS 'Ghostriders', activated 5 October 1989 as an operational F-117A unit with a 'Pacific' (Korea) wartime tasking. The 4452d TS inactivated on 30 May 1989 without gaining a new identity. Finally the 4453d TES became the 417th TFTS 'Bandits' as the F-117A RTU. The F-117-equipped 37th TFW was assigned to 12th AF.

The F-117A was considered for the 1986 Operation El Dorado Canyon strikes on Libya, but discounted for fear of revealing the secret programme; USAFE F-111Fs undertook the mission instead. Its combat debut came during Operation Just Cause in Panama. On the night of 19/20 December 1989, six 37th TFW F-117As flew directly from Tonopah to Panama, refuelling five times during the round trip. Two acted as spares. Two were to support a Special Operations 'snatch' operation targeting Panama's General Noriega, which was cancelled as they approached. The final pair dropped GBU-27s on a field near the Panamanian Defense Forces' Rio Hato barracks

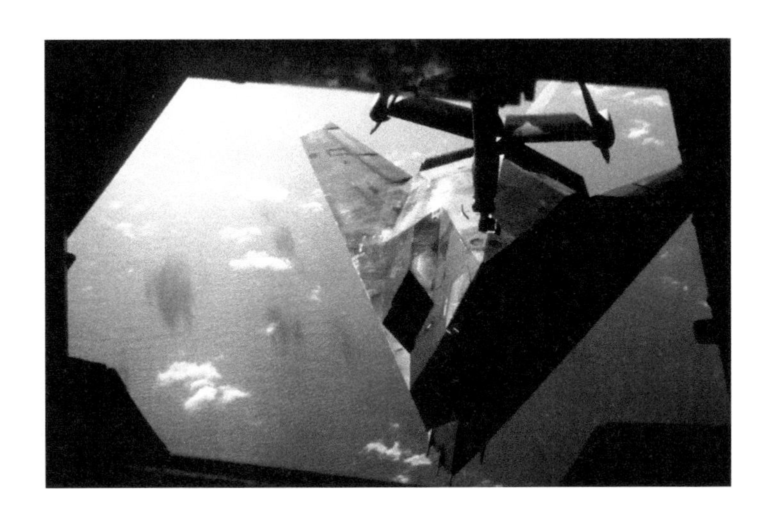

Following public acknowledgment and transfer of operations to the 37th TFW in 1989, an F-117A refuels from a KC-10A. (NARA)

to 'stun, disorient and confuse' the occupants prior to an assault by US Army Rangers; they missed their target by several hundred feet. After this inauspicious start, the F-117A would go on to see notable service after the Cold War's conclusion.

The Tactical Air Warfare Center (TAWC) at Eglin AFB ('ED', replaced by 'OT' from 1982 and black and white checkerboard tail markings) conducted operational testing and evaluation (OT&E) of all TAC aircraft, weapons and tactics. TAWC's 4485th TS operated a mixed fleet throughout the 1980s: A-10A (from 1980 to 1989, operating three in 1989), F-4E (throughout the decade, operating seven in 1989), RF-4C (throughout the decade, operating four in 1989), F-15A/B/C (throughout the decade, operating one F-15A/four F-15Cs in 1989) and F-16A/C (from 1980 and 1985 respectively, operating two F-16As/three F-16Cs in 1989). 'Det 3, TAWC' at Mountain Home AFB operated two 'OT' coded EF-111As from April 1979 to

A 4485th Test Squadron, TAWC, F-15A during 1987. (NARA)

Seen at George AFB during January 1987, this Det 5, TAWC, F-4G was the first to be painted in 'Hill Gray II' to evaluate the scheme's suitability for the Wild Weasel mission. A 562d TFTS F-4G, in hitherto standard 'European I' camouflage, is alongside for comparison. At this time, Det 5, TAWC's F-4Gs were pooled with the 562d TFTS, complete with 'WW' tail codes. Note the solid blue squadron colour of the 562d TFTS and blue checkerboard of Det 5, TAWC. Six months later Det 5, TAWC became autonomous with three 'OT' coded F-4Gs, remaining at George AFB. (NARA)

Another view of the 'European I' 562d TFTS and 'Hill Gray II' Det 5, TAWC F-4Gs at George AFB. 'Hill Gray II' was subsequently adopted across the fleet. In the background are 35th TFW F-4Es. (NARA)

December 1991, initially operating the pair of EF-111A prototypes with high visibility markings. 'Det 5, TAWC' activated 1 April 1980 with the F-4G at George AFB, initially using 'WW' coded aircraft pooled with the resident 562d TFTS, until becoming autonomous in July 1987 and gaining three 'OT' coded F-4Gs. On 1 July 1988 an intermediate 4443d Test and Evaluation Group activated under TAWC, controlling its component units. The Mountain Home and George TAWC Dets were redesignated 'Det 3, 4443d TEG' and 'Det 5, 4443d TEG' on 1 August 1988.

The Tactical Fighter Weapons Center (TFWC) at Nellis AFB, was concerned with advanced tactical training plus test and evaluation. It was assigned the large and varied 57th TTW at Nellis ('WA' and black/yellow checkerboard), which became the 57th FWW on 1 March 1980. The TFWC units made extensive use of the Nellis Air Force Range to the north and north-west of Nellis AFB. This huge range complex was described as being almost as large as Switzerland; aircraft could fly at supersonic speeds from 100 to 50,000 feet in the airspace above. Throughout were a number of bombing/gunnery and electronic warfare ranges. From 1985 a small ACMI range (subsequently expanded) was added to the Nellis ranges to provide for improved air combat training debriefing.

Until 1981 the 57th TTW/FWW controlled three Fighter Weapons Squadrons, providing graduate-level instructor fighter weapons courses; the 66th FWS with A-10As, the 414th FWS with F-4Es and the 433d FWS with F-15A/Bs. These inactivated on 30 December 1981, replaced by the USAF Fighter Weapons School, which controlled several 'Divisions': the 'A-10 Division' (with A-10As), the 'F-4 Division' (with F-4Es – it ceased operations 23 July 1985), the 'F-15 Division' (initially with F-15A/Bs, F-15C/Ds from August 1983) and the 'F-16 Division' (with F-16A/Bs, re-equipping with F-16C/D Block 32s during 1988/9). The Fighter Weapons School's Divisions shared the 422d TES aircraft. Det 1, USAF Fighter Weapons School activated January 1982. This was the former Det 2 57th FWW operating F-111As from Mountain Home; from June 1988 it moved to Cannon AFB with F-111Ds.

The 57th TTW/FWW also operated weapons and tactics OT&E units. The 422d FWS (which became the 422d TES on 30 December 1981) operated a number of Divisions: 'A-10 Division', 'F-4E Division' (until 1985), 'F-15 Division', 'F-15E Division' (from 1989) and the 'F-16 Division' (from 1980). As mentioned, the aircraft of the 422d TES Divisions were shared with the Fighter Weapons School Divisions.

The 431st FWS activated 1 October 1980 (becoming 431st TES 30 December 1981) with F-111D/E/Fs at McClellan AFB, California, replacing Det 3, 57th FWW. During the early 1980s it had three F-111Ds, four F-111Es and one F-111F.

Also under the wing was the USAF Air Demonstration Squadron, the 'Thunderbirds' air demonstration team, operating T-38As at the decade's onset. They lost four team pilots (including the leader) in a tragic training crash at Indian Springs Air Force Auxiliary Field (AFAF), Nevada on 18 January 1982; their 1982 display season was cancelled while the team rebuilt. As part of this process the team switched back to frontline fighters (having downgraded to trainers following the 1973 oil crisis) receiving F-16A/Bs from 22 June 1982.

The 4440th TFTG (Red Flag) administered 'Red Flag', the two-week complex and realistic air combat training exercises, held several times a year and attended by US and allied units.

The 57th TTW/FWW operated a number of Detachments.

Det 1, 57th TTW (Det 1, 57th FWW from 1 March 1980) operated a handful of white/red range support UH-1Ns, replaced by 4460th Helicopter Squadron (HS) 'Scorpions' (still under 57th FWW) which activated on 1 November 1983. The 4460th HS adopted a black/white scheme for the UH-1Ns. A new Det 1, 57th FWW

Two 57th FWW F-15As during May 1980. These were pooled for use by both the 433d FWS, which conducted graduate-level instructor fighter weapons courses, and the 422d FWS 'F-15 Division', which undertook weapons and tactics OT&E. (NARA)

A 57th FWW F-16A Block 10 during 1983. The fighter weapons training and OT&E units had been reorganised since the time of the previous image. Consequently these F-16s were pooled for use by the USAF Fighter Weapons School's 'F-16 Division' for graduate-level instructor fighter weapons courses and 422d TES 'F-16 Division' for weapons and tactics OT&E. (NARA)

A 57th FWW A-10A during 1988 with an early trial fit of 'Low Voltage Formation' (LVF) electroluminescent strips, or 'slime lights'. These glowed green, aiding night formation flying. They are seen on the forward fuselage sides, down the fin, forming a pair of chevrons behind the cockpit and an inverted 'T' on the wingtip. LVF strips were retrofitted to all A-10s from around 1990, although arranged slightly differently. This was at the same time as, but separate to, an A-10 upgrade program known as Low Altitude Safety and Targeting Enhancements (LASTE). LASTE included addition of radar altimeter, weapons delivery computer and an autopilot, improving safety and operational effectiveness. The 57th FWW A-10As were pooled for use by both the Fighter Weapons School's 'A-10 Division' and the 422d TES 'A-10 Division'. (NARA)

An early-production F-16C Block 25 of the 57th FWW (pooled for use by the FWS 'F-16 Division' and 422d TES 'F-16 Division') over Lake Mead, Nevada, during 1988, carrying a pair of CATM-9L/Ms. (NARA)

A 57th FWW F-15C over Lake Mead during 1988. These were pooled for use by both the Fighter Weapons School's 'F-15 Division' and the 422d TES 'F-15 Division'. (NARA)

A 431st TES, 57th FWW F-111D also over Lake Mead during 1988. (NARA)

A member of the USAF Air Demonstration Squadron, better known as the 'Thunderbirds', polishes one of the team's F-16As at Nellis AFB during early September 1982. The team had re-equipped with the F-16 just over two months earlier. (NARA)

The Thunderbirds performing their first display since re-equipping with the F-16, at Nellis AFB on 2 April 1983. (NARA)

operated from Luke AFB from 1 November 1985 until 5 October 1989, operating 'European One' camouflaged F-16C/Ds for CAS trials (part of the abortive scheme to replace A-10As with F-16s). This mission transferred to the 422d TES on 5 October 1989. On the latter date another Det 1, 57th FWW formed, flying F-117A test duties at Tonopah, replacing Det 2, 4450th TG ('R-Unit').

Det 2, 57th TTW (Det 2 57th FWW from 1 March 1980) operated F-111As at Mountain Home as the F-111 FWS. As mentioned this became Det 1, USAF Fighter Weapons School in January 1982. Following the MiG-equipped 4477th TES's inactivation, a new Det 2, 57th FWW formed, operating MiG-23s from Groom Lake.

Det 3, 57th TTW (Det 3, 57th FWW from 1 March 1980) operated F-111D/E/F from McClellan AFB for F-111 OT&E. As mentioned, this inactivated 1 October 1980, replaced by 431st FWS.

Det 16, 57th TTW (redesignated Det 16, 57th FWW 1 March 1980) at Hill AFB ('HL') conducted multinational F-16 OT&E between 1 August 1979 and 1 December 1981. Operating early model F-16A/Bs, including European partner nations' F-16s, and initially equipped with Block 1 jets, by January 1980 it had eight/two F-16A/B Block 5s (later receiving an F-16B Block 1 attrition replacement for a lost F-16B Block 5). Assigned European F-16s were in addition to these USAF airframes. The mission was later passed to the 422d FWS at Nellis.

During the Vietnam War period, TFWC produced the 'Red Baron' reports that studied air-to-air combat action between USAF and North Vietnamese fighters, aiming to improve the USAF's disappointing pilot proficiency. A key finding was the importance of Dissimilar Air Combat Training (DACT), i.e. air combat training against a different type with different performance characteristics. Hitherto most USAF air combat training was conducted within the unit, with identical aircraft flown against each other. The resulting Aggressor programme envisaged using a dissimilar type, flown by pilots employing enemy tactics, for air-to-air training of frontline units. Around the same time Israel passed on to the USAF three captured MiGs for trials; a MiG-21F-13 (codenamed 'HAVE DOUGHNUT') and a pair of MiG-17Fs ('HAVE DRILL' and 'HAVE FERRY'). FERRY was permanently loaned, DOUGHNUT and DRILL temporarily. These were used by the Foreign Technology Division (FTD) of Air Force Systems Command (AFSC) at Groom Lake, Nevada, for 'technical exploitation' (evaluating their performance) as well as 'operational exploitation' (testing them against US fighters). Those developing the Aggressor programme were keen to use genuine MiGs for that programme too. However, the secrecy surrounding the MiGs and their limited numbers precluded this. Therefore the Aggressors were initially established (64th FWS) with stopgap T-38As in exotic 'enemy-style' camouflage schemes. F-5Es built for South Vietnam, but not delivered when the Vietnam War ended, plus others that escaped to Thailand during the Saigon-regime's final downfall, resulted in over 100 F-5Es becoming available. These F-5Es (a respectable MiG-21 simulator) were soon used to replace the T-38As and a second squadron (65th FWS) was equipped.

They wore 'Soviet-style' two-digit, or occasionally three-digit, 'Bort' numbers. From around 1980 the 64th used red 'Bort numbers' and the 65th used blue 'Borts'. However, it appears that later the aircraft were pooled between both squadrons. During the 1980s over sixty-five F-5Es were assigned to the two squadrons. As well as providing core hostile 'red air' at exercises like Red Flag, the Aggressors main role was touring fighter bases nationally, providing air combat training. Up to a third of the Aggressors were so deployed at any one time, with a typical individual deployment consisting of around six F-5Es.

A 64th FWS F-5E 'Aggressor' in 57th FWW flagship markings during 1980, carrying wingtip AIM-9Js. (NARA)

The 57th FWW flagship F-5E is in 'Old Blue', one of many Aggressor schemes. It consisted of FS 35164 Intermediate Blue, FS 35190 Pastel Blue and FS 35414 Light Blue with FS 35622 Duck Egg Blue undersides. (NARA)

Six 57th FWW Aggressor F-5Es while deployed to Seymour Johnson AFB during 1985 for DACT with the resident 4th TFW. Illustrating the variety of camouflage schemes, the first three aircraft are 74-1528 'Red 28' in 'New Lizard' camouflage, 74-1505 'Red 05' in 'Old Ghost' and 72-1417 'Red 17' in 'Flogger'. (NARA)

The 64th FWS was redesignated the 64th Tactical Fighter Training Aggressor Squadron (TFTAS) on 30 December 1981 and 64th Aggressor Squadron (AS) 1 April 1983. Its F-5Es gained 'WA' tail codes and black/yellow checkerboard markings in the mid-1980s. It briefly added a pair of two-seat F-5Fs alongside its F-5Es in the mid-1980s. An investigation following an Aggressor F-5F crash (from which the pilot safely ejected) concluded that F-5Fs were unsuitable for Aggressor use as they departed controlled flight more easily than F-5Es; they were withdrawn and transferred to the 425th TFTS at Williams – it is worth noting, however, that the Navy successfully operated F-5Fs in its similar Adversary programme. The 64th briefly replaced its F-5Es with F-16A Block 10s from April 1988, receiving at least twelve jets from the co-located 474th TFW (primarily from 430th TFS) as that wing drew down. These F-16As retained their standard grey camouflage and did not receive Aggressor schemes. From April 1989 the unit re-equipped with eighteen factory-new F-16C Block 32s, wearing 'Flogger' and 'Fulcrum' schemes, based on typical MiG-23 and MiG-29 camouflage.

The 65th FWS 'Aggressors', redesignated 65th TFTAS 30 December 1981 and 65th AS 1 April 1983, also briefly acquired a pair of F-5Fs mid-decade, likewise belatedly adopting 'WA' codes and black/yellow checkerboard tail markings around the same time. While the 64th AS upgraded to F-16s, the rest of the Aggressor programme (not only the 65th AS, but also USAFE's 527th AS and PACAF's 26th AS) was curtailed due to the USAF's funding drawdown. Consequently the 65th AS did not receive F-16s and inactivated on 7 April 1989.

While there had initially been unrealistic hopes of forming the Aggressor squadrons with genuine enemy equipment, such training later became possible as more Soviet-designed aircraft clandestinely came into US possession. This allowed for some to be allocated to TAC for air-to-air combat training 'exposures' of frontline USAF (and USN/USMC) aircrew under the CONSTANT PEG programme. The 4477th Test and Evaluation Flight (TEF) (later named 'Red Eagles') activated on 1 April 1977. While assigned to the 57th TTW at Nellis, it established itself at Tonopah TRA at the far north-western corner of the Nellis ranges. As mentioned, facilities were initially very spartan and slowly developed. The 'exposures' took the form of an initial formation flight with the MiGs to allow the frontline pilot to get over what was described as the 'buck fever' of simply seeing a MiG in the air and subsequently moved on to more complex DACT engagements. The unit was redesignated 4477th TES on 1 March 1980. The Department of the Navy funded 30 percent of CONSTANT PEG, consequently a proportion of the unit's pilots came from the USN/USMC. The 'Red Eagles' maintained strong links with AFSC's 6513th TES 'Red Hats' at Groom Lake, which conducted evaluation of Soviet aircraft.

By 1981 the 4477th TES-operated three MiG-17F (some, or all, likely ex-Indonesian Air Force, Polish-built, Lim-5s), six MiG-21F-13 (ex-Indonesian) and one MiG-23BN (ex-Egyptian). The MiG-17Fs were grounded after a non-fatal accident on 8 April 1982, subsequently made permanent as the type was no longer deemed to represent a viable threat. By December 1983 they operated six MiG-21F-13, three MiG-21MF (possibly ex-Egyptian), two MiG-23BN and four MiG-23MS (ex-Egyptian). In December 1985 they reached peak MiG strength with seventeen MiG-21s and ten MiG-23s. In 1987 the elderly MiG-21F-13s were replaced by a batch of twelve factory-new Chengdu F-7B (Chinese MiG-21 copies) either bought directly from China or via Egypt. However that year they operated fourteen 'MiG-21s', so as well as the twelve F-7Bs it is possible that the additional two airframes were MiG-21MFs.

Ten MiG-23 were still in use at this time. These number remained static (although the MiG-23s reduced to nine) at the time the unit ceased operations on 4 March 1988, a decision arrived upon at short notice due to the aforementioned funding drawdown. The 4477th also leased support aircraft to fly personnel from Nellis to Tonopah, initially using a Cessna 207, replaced in 1978 by Cessna 404s, these being replaced by Mitsubishi MU-2s from 3 October 1981 until they were relinquished on 8 February 1985. The 4477th also operated a pair of T-38s from 1979, increased to four from 8 February 1985 and five by 1988 (a mixture of T-38A and AT-38B models). Although it ceased operations in 1988, the 4477th didn't formally inactivate until 15 July 1990. As mentioned above, following inactivation of the 'Red Eagles', a new Det 2, 57th FWW formed operating MiG-23s (but no MiG-21s/F-7Bs) from Groom Lake. This involved a small number of aircraft and crews, allowing MiG-23-qualified TAC pilots to maintain the minimum hours required for currency. This did not allow for exposures to frontline crews as previously done by the 4477th TES, but allowed TAC to maintain the ability to reactivate the MiG exposure program in due course if and when funding allowed.

The other wing that fell under the TFWC was the 554th Operations Support Wing (OSW) at Indian Springs AFAF. It controlled the 554th Range Group which operated the Nellis ranges. The 4460th HS 'Scorpions' of the 57th FWW with its white/black painted range support UH-1Ns were reassigned to the 554th OSW on 1 June 1985, subsequently inactivating 31 December 1987.

The 552d Airborne Warning and Control Wing (AWACW) was reactivated on 1 July 1976 at Tinker AFB, Oklahoma, having briefly been inactivated (as a Group) after relinquishing its previous EC-121 Warning Star aircraft. The wing would operate the new E-3A Sentry 'AWACS' and would also have other squadrons assigned operating specialist types. The wing's first two E-3A squadrons activated on 1 July 1976; 963d Airborne Warning and Control Squadron (AWACS) (black/white checkerboard tail colours) and 966th Airborne Warning and Control Training Squadron (AWACTS) (blue), the E-3 RTU. From 1985 the 966th added a pair of leased Boeing 707s, later purchased and redesignated TC-18E, to act as flight deck transition and air refuelling trainers. The 964th AWACS (red) activated on 1 July 1977 and the 965th AWACS (yellow) activated on 1 July 1978. The 960th Airborne Warning and Control Support Squadron (AWACSS), activated on 1 September 1979 (redesignated 960th AWACS on 1 January 1982), was detached at Keflavik, Iceland. It had no aircraft assigned, but controlled temporary duty E-3s (usually a pair) rotationally deployed to Iceland by the Tinker squadrons. The 961st AWACSS, activated 1 October 1979 (redesignated 961st AWACS on 1 January 1982) likewise supported rotational E-3s deployed to Kadena Air Base, Okinawa. Other units assigned to the 552d AWACW were as follows. The 7th ACCS (detached at Keesler AFB, Oklahoma, periodically using 'KS') was reassigned to the wing on 1 October 1976 and operated the EC-130E (ABCCC) Airborne Battlefield Command and Control Center. The EC-130E (ABCCC) featured a removable AN/ASC-15 command battle staff module in the cargo bay, accommodating up to sixteen operators and command staff. As noted, three EC-130E (ABCCC)s were used as ground tankers during Operation Eagle Claw, chosen due to their air-to-air refuelling capability; a pair of 3000lb fuel bladders replaced each aircraft's battle staff module. One aircraft was lost in the ground collision with the RH-53D at Desert One. The 8th Tactical Deployment Control Squadron (TDCS) at Tinker AFB operated two EC-135K aircraft which primarily conducted the 'HEAD DANCER' mission, acting as

A 41st ECS EC-130H 'Compass Call' at Davis-Monthan AFB during Gallant Eagle '86. The tail-mounted wire antenna arrays are apparent here. This EC-130H retains the MAC version of 'European I', rather than the more usual EC-130H two-tone grey scheme. MAC 'European I' replaced the FS 36081 grey of TAC 'European I' with slightly lighter FS 36118 grey. The usual EC-130H two-tone grey camouflage was the same scheme worn by EF-111As. (NARA)

a command post for fighters making global deployments. During 1982 the EC-135Ks J57-P/F-43W turbojets were replaced by more efficient TF33-PW-102 turbofans. On 26 October 1983 a TF33-P-5 powered C-135E transport, used as the executive transport of Commander TAC, was added to the unit. The 41st ECS, detached at Davis-Monthan AFB, operated the EC-130H 'Compass Call' communications jamming aircraft. Although activated on 1 July 1980 it did not receive its first aircraft until 19 March 1982. Initially using 'DM' codes, it dropped these in the mid-1980s, occasionally displaying a tail stripe featuring small lightning bolts.

The wing's responsibilities had become so wide that it was redesignated the 552d Airborne Warning and Control Division on 1 October 1983. There was further reorganisation on 1 April 1985 as the 552d reverted to wing status, and the 28th Air Division was activated at Tinker. Henceforth, the 552d AWACW, which previously reported directly to TAC HQ, was reassigned to 28th AD and the latter reported directly to TAC. Furthermore, on the same date the 7th ACCS and 41st ECS were reassigned from 552d AWACW to 28th AD. On 1 March 1986 the 8th TDCS was also reassigned to 28th AD. This left 552d AWACW responsible only for the E-3 squadrons. Finally on 1 July 1986 the 962d AWACS was activated under the 552d at Elmendorf AFB, Alaska supporting E-3s rotationally deployed there.

The USAF received thirty-four E-3As in two sub types; the first twenty-four were 'Core E-3A' with AN/APY-1 radar, the last ten were 'Standard E-3A' with AN/APY-2. Progressively upgraded from the mid-1980s, the 'Cores' became E-3Bs and 'Standards' became E-3Cs. The first E-3B was redelivered to the 552d on 19 July 1984. The E-3B added the faster IBM CC-2 computer, ECM-resistant communications, limited maritime surveillance capability, more radios, five additional display consoles and

'Have Quick' secure communications. E-3Cs added slightly larger crew capacity, five additional display consoles and 'Have Quick'.

The 552d's E-3s were active supporting various operations during the decade. In September 1980 four E-3s and crews deployed to Riyadh, Saudi Arabia under 'ELF One' (European Liaison Force One) to augment Royal Saudi Air Force air defence radar coverage during the Iran–Iraq War. The eight-year deployment, initially under USAFE control, passed to CENTAF control upon the latter's creation on 1 January 1983. Between 1981 and 1983 E-3s made periodic deployments to Cairo West, Egypt and Khartoum, Sudan, due to Libyan intervention in Chad. Four E-3As participated in Operation Urgent Fury over Grenada in 1983. E-3s also supported the 1986 Operation El Dorado Canyon USAFE/USN strikes on Libya and Operation Just Cause in Panama in 1989.

*Left*: A 552d AWACW E-3A deployed to Howard AFB, Panama, during Exercise Black Fury II in 1979. (NARA)

*Below*: Two 965th AWACS, 552d AWACW E-3Cs deployed to Cairo West AB, Egypt, during Bright Star '85. A row of KC-135Es are in the background, the nearest being from 126th AREFS, 128th AREFG, Wisconsin ANG. (NARA)

A 552d AWACW E-3 during Solid Shield '87. (NARA)

Airman Eric Roberts of the 363d Security Police Squadron talks with Airman Michael Bailey of the 552d Aircraft Generation Squadron while on sentry duty during Shadow Hawk '87, a phase of Bright Star '87 at Azraq Air Base, Jordan. (NARA)

# End of an Era

The Cold War's abrupt conclusion resulted in a 'peace dividend' that considerably cut USAF budgets. The inactivation of units was delayed by the Gulf crisis and war in 1990/1, but got underway in earnest immediately afterwards. In 1992 the USAF was completely reorganised and the familiar MAJCOMs ceased to exist.

Air Combat Command (ACC) was activated on 1 June 1992, replacing TAC, while absorbing all of SAC's former bombers and ICBMs plus some of its tankers. ACC also absorbed some of MAC's former C-130 tactical transports. The reorganisation recognised the increasingly blurred lines between 'tactical' and 'strategic' air power in the post-Cold War world, as demonstrated in the Gulf War. During the latter B-52G 'strategic' bombers bombed forward enemy troop positions while 'tactical' jets hit 'strategic' targets in Iraq (although this was not a new phenomenon; similar had occurred in Vietnam). The reorganisation saw several wings become multi-type composite wings, better suited to 'expeditionary' warfare. Over the following years the USAF continued to shrink and ACC would further reorganise. In 1993 ICBMs were transferred to Air Force Space Command, ACC's RTUs transferred to Air Education and Training Command and most ACC tankers were transferred to Air Mobility Command. Meanwhile remaining US-based tactical transports transferred to ACC (later transferred back out of ACC in 1997). By the late 1990s composite wings reverted to single-type wings. Air Force Global Strike Command activated on 7 August 2009 as a successor to SAC; over a period of years thereafter it would absorb all of ACC's bombers (and Space Command's ICBMs). Consequently, at the time of writing ACC has returned to an organisation much more reminiscent of TAC which it replaced.

# Bibliography

Bell, Dana, *USAF Colors and Markings in the 1990s* (London: Lionel Leventhal Limited, 1992)

Donald, David (Ed.), *US Air Force Air Power Directory* (London: Aerospace Publishing Limited, 1992)

Francillon, René J., *The United States Air National Guard* (London: Aerospace Publishing Limited, 1993)

Cole, Ronald H, *Operation Urgent Fury* (Washington: Joint History Office, Office of the Chairman of the Joint Chiefs of Staff, 1997)

Donald, David and Lake, Jon (Eds.), *Encyclopedia of World Military Aircraft Volumes 1 & 2* (London: Aerospace Publishing Limited, 1994)

Hopkins III, Robert S., *The Boeing KC-135 Stratotanker: More Than a Tanker* (Manchester: Crécy Publishing Limited, 2018)

Lake, Jon (Ed.), *McDonnell F-4 Phantom: Spirit in the Sky* (London: Aerospace Publishing Limited, 1992)

Martin, Patrick, *Tail Code: The Complete History of USAF Tactical Aircraft Tail Code Markings* (Atglen: Schiffer Publishing Limited, 1994)

Peake, William R., *McDonnell Douglas F-4 Phantom II Production and Operational Data* (Hinckley: Midland Publishing, 2004)

Rogers, Brian, *United States Air Force Unit Designations since 1978* (Hinckley: Midland Publishing, 2005)

Thigpen, Jerry, *The Praetorian STARShip: The Untold Story of the Combat Talon* (Maxwell AFB: Air University Press, 2001)

Thornborough, Anthony M. and Davies, Peter E., *The Phantom Story* (London: Arms and Armour Press, 1994)

Yenne, Bill, *The Complete History of US Cruise Missiles* (Forest Lake: Specialty Press, 2018)

## Journals and periodicals

*World Air Power Journal*, various volumes (Aerospace Publishing Limited)

## Unpublished papers

Eldredge, Major Maurice C., *A Brief History of 'ADTAC': The First Five Years* (Maxwell AFB: Air Command and Staff College, Air University, 1985)

Morrison, Blake (Ed.), *USAF Fighter Weapons Review: Winter 86* (Nellis AFB: Commandant USAF Fighter Weapons School, 57th Fighter Weapins Wing, 1986)
Stiles, Gerald J., *The Wild Weasel Development Programs: One Run, One Hit, One Error* (Santa Monica: The RAND Corporation, 1990)

## Website

http://www.sharpshooter-maj.com

# Appendix I

# TAC Structure January 1980

HQ Langley AFB, VA

## Direct Reporting

**4450th TG** (A-unit) (Tonopah Test Range, NV) [1]
Det 1, 4450th TG ('Q-Unit')
Det 2, 4450th TG ('R-Unit') (Burbank, CA/Groom Lake, NV)

**Tactical Air Warfare Center (TAWC)** (Eglin AFB, FL, 'ED', black/white checkerboard)
4485th TS – A-10A, RF-4C, F-4E, F-15A, F-16A
Det 3, TAWC – EF-111A (Mountain Home)

**Tactical Fighter Weapons Center (TFWC)** (Nellis AFB, NV)
**57th TTW** (Nellis AFB, NV, 'WA', black/yellow checkerboard)
Det 1, 57th TTW – UH-1N (Indian Springs AFAF, NV)
Det 2, 57th TTW – F-111As (Mountain Home AFB, ID)
Det 3, 57th TTW – F-111D/E/F (McClellan AFB, CA)
Det 16, 57th TTW – F-16A/B (Hill AFB, UT, 'HL')
64th FWS – F-5E
65th FWS – F-5E
66th FWS – A-10A
414th FWS – F-4E
433d FWS – F-15A/B
422d FWS:
'A-10 Division' – A-10A
'F-4E Division' – F-4E
'F-15 Division' – F-15A/B
'F-16 Division' – F-16A/B
USAF Air Demonstration Squadron ('Thunderbirds') – T-38A
4477th TEF – MiG-17F, MiG-21, T-38A, Cessna 404 (Tonopah Test Range, NV)

**552d AWACW** (Tinker AFB, OK)
7th ACCS – EC-130E (ABCCC) (Keesler AFB, OK)
8th TDCS – EC-135K
960th AWACSS (Keflavik, Iceland – TDY E-3As)
961st AWACSS (Kadena AB, Okinawa – TDY E-3As)
963d AWACS – E-3A (black/white checkerboard)
964th AWACS – E-3A (red)
965th AWACS – E-3A (yellow)
966th AWACTS – E-3A (blue)

***USAF Southern Air Division*** (Howard AFB, Panama)
**24th CW** (Howard AFB, Panama)
24th CS – O-2A, UH-1N

## ADTAC, Peterson AFB, CO

***20th Air Division*** (Fort Lee AFS, VA)
48th FIS – F-106A/B, T-33A (Langley AFB, VA)

***21st Air Division*** (Hancock Field, NY)
49th FIS – F-106A/B, T-33A (Griffiss AFB, NY)

***23d Air Division*** (Duluth IAP, MN)
87th FIS – F-106A/B, T-33A (K.I. Sawyer AFB, MI)

**4787th ABG** – T-33A (Duluth IAP, MN)

***24th Air Division*** (Malmstrom AFB, MT)
5th FIS – F-106A/B, T-33A (Minot AFB, ND)
24th ADS – T-33A (Malmstrom AFB, MT)

***25th Air Division*** (McChord AFB, WA)
318th FIS – F-106A/B, T-33A (McChord AFB, WA)

***26th Air Division*** (Luke AFB, AZ)
84th FIS – F-106A/B, T-33A (Castle AFB, CA)
26th ADS – T-33A (Luke AFB, AZ)

***Air Forces Iceland*** (Keflavik, Iceland)
57th FIS – F-4E (NAS Keflavik, Iceland) (black/white checkerboard)

***Air Defense Weapons Center*** (Tyndall AFB, FL) ('Stars and Stripes' rudder markings)
2d FITS – F-106A/B, F-101B/F
95th FITS – T-33A
475th TS – F-106A/B, F-101B/F, EF-101B

## Ninth Air Force, Shaw AFB, SC

**1st TFW** (Langley AFB, VA, 'FF') (UH-1Ps attached to wing HQ)
27th TFS – F-15A/B (yellow)
71st TFS – F-15A/B (red)
94th TFS – F-15A/B (blue)
6th ACCS – EC-135P

**4th TFW** (Seymour Johnson AFB, NC, 'SJ')
334th TFS – F-4E (blue)
335th TFS – F-4E (green)
336th TFS – F-4E (yellow)

**23d TFW** (England AFB, LA, 'EL')
74th TFS – A-7D (blue)
75th TFS – A-7D (black/white)
76th TFS – A-7D (red)

**31st TFW** (Homestead AFB, FL, 'ZF')
306th TFTS – F-4D (yellow)
307th TFS – F-4E (red)
308th TFS – F-4E (green)
309th TFS – F-4E (blue)

**33d TFW** (Eglin AFB, FL, 'EG')
58th TFS – F-15C/D (blue)
59th TFS – F-15C/D (yellow)
60th TFS – F-15C/D (red)

**56th TFW** (MacDill AFB, FL, 'MC') (UH-1Ps attached to wing HQ)
13th TFTS – F-4D (black)
61st TFTS – F-16A/B Block 1/5 (yellow)
62nd TFS – F-4D (blue)
63d TFS – F-4D (red)

**347th TFW** (Moody AFB, GA, 'MY')
68th TFS – F-4E (red)
70th TFS – F-4E (blue/white)
339th TFS – F-4E (Silver)

**354th TFW** (Myrtle Beach AFB, SC, 'MB')
353d TFS – A-10A (red)
355th TFS – A-10A (white/blue)
356th TFS – A-10A (green)

**363d TRW** (Shaw AFB, SC, 'JO')
16th TRS – RF-4C (multi-red/yellow/black/white)
33d TRTS – RF-4C (blue)
62d TRS – RF-4C (red)

**507th TAIRCW** (Shaw AFB, SC, 'VA')
21st TASS – O-2A (black), OV-10A (no colour)
703d TASS(H) – CH-3E

**549th TASTG** (Patrick AFB, FL)
549th TASTS – O-2A, OV-10A

**1st SOW** (Hurlburt Field, FL)
8th SOS – MC-130E
16th SOS – AC-130H
20th SOS – CH-3E/UH-1N.

## Twelfth Air Force, Bergstrom AFB, TX

**27th TFW** (Cannon AFB, NM, 'CC')
481st TFTS – F-111D (green)
522d TFS – F-111D (red)
523d TFS – F-111D (blue)
524th TFS – F-111D (yellow)

**67th TRW** (Bergstrom AFB, TX, 'BA')
12th TRS – RF-4C (orange)
91st TRS – RF-4C (red)

**366th TFW** (Mountain Home AFB, ID, 'MO')
389th TFTS – F-111A (yellow)
390th TFS – F-111A (green)
391st TFS – F-111A (blue)

**388th TFW** (Hill AFB, UT, 'HL')
4th TFS – F-4D (yellow)
16th TFTS – F-16A/B Block 1/5/10 (blue)
34th TFS – F-16A/B Block 1/5/10 (red)
421st TFS – Nil (black) [2]

**474th TFW** (Nellis AFB, NV, 'NA')
428th TFS – F-4D (blue)
429th TFS – F-4D (yellow)
430th TFS – F-4D (red)

**602d TAIRCW** (Bergstrom AFB, TX)
23d TASS – O-2A (red or yellow), OV-10A (no colour)
27th TASS – O-2A (blue or red) (Davis-Monthan AFB, AZ)
701st TASS(H) – CH-3C (Bergstrom AFB, TX)

***Tactical Training, George*** (George AFB, CA):

**35th TFW** (George AFB, CA) (UH-1Ps attached to wing HQ)
20th TFTS – F-4E (blue, 'GA') (Luftwaffe aircraft)
21st TFTS – F-4E (black, 'GA')
39th TFTS – F-4G (white, 'WW')
561st TFS – F-4E (yellow, 'GA')
562d TFS – F-105G (green, 'GA'/'WW')
563d TFS – F-4G (red, 'WW')

***Tactical Training, Luke*** (Luke AFB, AZ):

**58th TTW** (Luke AFB, AZ)
69th TFTS – F-104G/TF-104G (Luftwaffe aircraft)
310th TFTS – F-4C (green, 'LA')
311th TFTS – F-4C (blue, 'LA')
426th TFTS – F-4C (yellow, 'LA')

**405th TTW** (Luke AFB, AZ) (UH-1F/P attached to wing HQ)
425th TFTS – F-5B/E/F (Williams AFB, AZ)
461st TFTS – F-15A/B (yellow, 'LA')
550th TFTS – F-15A/B (black/silver, 'LA')
555th TFTS – F-15A/B (green, 'LA')

***Tactical Training, Holloman*** (Holloman AFB, NM):

**49th TFW** (Holloman AFB, NM, 'HO')
7th TFS – F-15A/B (blue)
8th TFS – F-15A/B (yellow)
9th TFS – F-15A/B (red)

**479th TTW** (Holloman AFB, NM, 'HM')
416th TFTS – AT-38B (silver)
434th TFTS – AT-38B (red)
435th TFTS – AT-38B (blue)
436th TFTS – AT-38B (yellow)

**Tactical Training, Davis Monthan** (Davis Monthan AFB, AZ):

**355th TTW** (Davis Monthan AFB, AZ, 'DM')
333d TFTS – A-10A (red)
357th TFTS – A-10A (yellow)
358th TFTS – A-10A (green)

Notes:
1) No F-117s delivered until 1982.
2) Non-operational until Aug 1980 whilst awaiting F-16A/B.

# Appendix II

# TAC Structure January 1989

HQ Langley AFB, VA

## Direct Reporting

**4450th TG** (A-unit) (Tonopah Test Range, NV)
Det 2, 4450th TG ('R-Unit') Palmdale, CA/Groom Lake, NV
4450th TS ('I-Unit') – F-117A
4451st TS ('P-Unit') – A-7D/K (Nellis AFB, NV, 'LV'/black)
4452d TS ('Q-Unit') – F-117A
4453d TES ('Z-Unit') – F-117A

**Tactical Air Warfare Center (TAWC)** (Eglin AFB, FL, 'OT', black/white checkerboard)
**4443d TEG**
4485th TS – A-10A, RF-4C, F-4E, F-15A/C, F-16A/C
Det 3, 4443d TEG – EF-111A (Mountain Home)
Det 5, 4443d TEG – F-4G (George AFB, CA)

**Tactical Fighter Weapons Center (TFWC)** (Nellis AFB, NV)
**57th FWW** (Nellis AFB, NV, 'WA', black/yellow checkerboard)
Det 1, 57th FWW – F-16C/D Block 25 (Luke AFB)
Det 2, 57th FWW – MiG-23 (Groom Lake)
422d TES:
'A-10 Division' – A-10A
'F-15 Division' – F-15C/D
'F-15E Division' – F-15E
'F-16 Division' – F-16C/D Block 32
431st TES – F-111D/E/F (McClellan AFB, CA)
USAF Air Demonstration Squadron ('Thunderbirds') – F-16A/B Block 15
64th AS – F-16A Block 10
65th AS – F-5E
4477th TES [1]
USAF Fighter Weapons School:
'A-10 Division' – A-10A
'F-15 Division' – F-15C/D
'F-16 Division' – F-16C/D Block 32
Det 1, USAF Fighter Weapons School – F-111D (Cannon AFB, NM)

***28th Air Division*** (Tinker AFB, OK):
7th ACCS – EC-130E (ABCCC) (Keesler AFB, OK, 'KS')
8th TDCS – EC-135K, C-135E (Tinker AFB, OK)
41st ECS – EC-130H (Davis Monthan AFB, AZ)

**552d AWACW** (Tinker AFB, OK)
960th AWACS – (TDY E-3s) (NAS Keflavik, Iceland)
961st AWACS – (TDY E-3s) (Kadena AB, Okinawa)
962d AWACS – (TDY E-3s) (Elmendorf AFB, AK)
963d AWACS – E-3B/C (black/white checkerboard)
964th AWACS – E-3B/C (red)
965th AWACS – E-3B/C (yellow)
966th AWACTS – E-3B/C, TC-18E (blue)

## First Air Force Langley AFB, VA

***24th Air Division*** Griffiss AFB, NY
**SEADS** Tyndall AFB, FL:
48 FIS – F-15A/B (Langley AFB, VA, 'LY')
**NEADS** Griffiss AFB, NY

***25th Air Division*** McChord AFB, WA
**SWADS** March AFB, CA
**NWADS** McChord AFB, WA:
318th FIS – F-15A/B (blue) (McChord AFB, WA, 'TC')

***Air Forces Iceland*** (Keflavik, Iceland)
57th FIS – F-15C/D (NAS Keflavik, Iceland) ('IS', black/white checkerboard)

***United States Air Force Air Defense Weapons Center (ADWC)*** (Tyndall AFB, FL):

**325th TTW** (Tyndall AFB, FL, 'TY')
1st TFTS – F-15A/B (red)
2d TFTS – F-15A/B (yellow)
95th TFTS – F-15A/B (blue)

**475th WEG** (Tyndall AFB, FL)
82d TATS – QF-100D/F, MQM-107B/D, BQM-34A/F

## Ninth Air Force, Shaw AFB, SC

**1st TFW** (Langley AFB, VA, 'FF')
27th TFS – F-15C/D (yellow)
71st TFS – F-15C/D (red)
94th TFS – F-15C/D (blue)
6th ACCS – EC-135P
4401st HF – UH-1N

**4th TFW** (Seymour Johnson AFB, NC, 'SJ')
334th TFS – F-4E (blue)
335th TFS – F-4E (green)
336th TFS – F-4E (yellow)

**23d TFW** (England AFB, LA, 'EL')
74th TFS – A-10A (blue)
75th TFS – A-10A (black/white)
76th TFS – A-10A (red)

**31st TFW** (Homestead AFB, FL, 'HS')
307th TFS – F-16A/B Block 15 (red)
308th TFS – F-16A/B Block 15 (green)
309th TFS – F-16A/B Block 15 (blue)

**33d TFW** (Eglin AFB, FL, 'EG')
58th TFS – F-15C/D (blue)
59th TFS – F-15C/D (yellow)
60th TFS – F-15C/D (red)

**56th TTW** (MacDill AFB, FL, 'MC')
61st TFTS – F-16A/B Block 10, F-16C/D Block 30 (yellow) [2]
62d TFTS – F-16A/B Block 10, F-16C/D Block 30 (blue) [2]
63d TFTS – F-16A/B Block 10, F-16C/D Block 30 (red) [2]
72d TFTS – F-16A/B Block 10 (black)

**347th TFW** (Moody AFB, GA, 'MY')
68th TFS – F-16A/B Block 15 (red)
69th TFS – F-16A/B Block 15 (silver)
70th TFS – F-16A/B Block 15 (blue/white)

**354th TFW** (Myrtle Beach AFB, SC, 'MB')
353d TFS – A-10A (red)
355th TFS – A-10A (blue)
356th TFS – A-10A (green)

**363d TFW** (Shaw AFB, SC, 'SW')
16th TRS – RF-4C (red/yellow/white/black)
17th TFS – F-16C/D Block 25 (white)
19th TFS – F-16C/D Block 25 (yellow)
33d TFS – F-16C/D Block 25 (blue)

**507th TAIRCW** (Shaw AFB, SC, 'SR')
21st TASS OV-10A (blue/yellow)

## Twelfth Air Force, Bergstrom AFB, TX

**27th TFW** (Cannon AFB, NM, 'CC')
522d TFS – F-111D (red)
523d TFS – F-111D (blue)
524th TFTS – F-111D (yellow)

**67th TRW** (Bergstrom AFB, TX, 'BA')
12th TRS – RF-4C (orange)

45th TRTS – RF-4C (blue)
62d TRTS – RF-4C (yellow)
91st TRS – RF-4C (red)

**366th TFW** (Mountain Home AFB, ID, 'MO')
389th TFTS – F-111A (yellow)
390th ECS – EF-111A
391st TFS – F-111A (blue)

**388th TFW** (Hill AFB, UT, 'HL')
4th TFS – F-16A/B Block 15 (yellow)
34th TFS – F-16A/B Block 15 (red)
421st TFS – F-16A/B Block 15 (black)

**474th TFW** (Nellis AFB, NV, 'NA')
428th TFS – F-16A/B Block 10 (blue)
429th TFS – F-16A/B Block 10 (black)
430th TFS – F-16A/B Block 10 (red)

***830th Air Division*** (Howard AFB, Panama):

**24th CW** (Howard AFB, Panama, 'HW')
24th TASS – OA-37B (blue)

***831st Air Division*** (George AFB, CA):

**35th TTW** (George AFB, CA, 'GA')
20th TFTS – F-4E (silver) (Luftwaffe aircraft)
21st TFTS – F-4E (black)

**37th TFW** (George AFB, CA, 'WW')
561st TFS – F-4E/G (yellow)
562d TFTS – F-4E/G (blue)
563d TFS – F-4E/G (red)

***832d Air Division*** (Luke AFB, AZ):

**58th TTW** (Luke AFB, AZ, 'LF')
310th TFS – F-16A/B Block 10 (green/gold)
311th TFS – F-16A/B Block 10 (blue/white)
312th TFS – F-16C/D Block 25 (black/red)
314th TFS – F-16C/D Block 25 (yellow/black)

**405th TTW** (Luke AFB, AZ, 'LA')
425th TFTS – F-5B/E/F (detached at Williams AFB, AZ)
426th TFTS – F-15A/B/D (red)
461st TFTS – F-15E (black/yellow)
550th TFTS – F-15A/B (black/silver) (To F-15E March 1989)
555th TFTS – F-15A/B (green)

***833d Air Division*** (Holloman AFB, NM):

**49th TFW** (Holloman AFB, NM, 'HO')
7th TFS – F-15A/B (blue)
8th TFS – F-15A/B (yellow)
9th TFS – F-15A/B (red)

**479th TTW** (Holloman AFB, NM, 'HM')
433d TFTS – AT-38B (green)
434th TFTS – AT-38B (red)
435th TFTS – AT-38B (blue)
436th TFTS – AT-38B (yellow)

***836th Air Division*** (Davis Monthan AFB, AZ):

**355th TTW** (Davis Monthan AFB, AZ, 'DM')
333d TFTS – A-10A (red)
357th TFTS – A-10A (yellow)
358th TFTS – A-10A (green)

**602d TAIRCW** (Davis Monthan AFB, AZ)
22d TASTS – OA-10A, OV-10A (yellow, 'NF')
23d TASS – OA-10A (blue, 'NF')
27th TASS – OV-10A (yellow/blue) (George AFB, CA, 'VV')

**868th TMTG** (Davis Monthan AFB, AZ)
868th TMTS – BGM-109G training unit

Notes:
1) Had ceased operations but was yet to inactivate.
2) Transitioning from F-16A/B Block 10 to F-16C/D Block 30.